FROM CRUTCHES
TO CRUSHING IT

FROM CRUTCHES TO CRUSHING IT

ISBN: 978-0-7961-2787-7 (Hardcover)
ISBN: 978-0-7961-2788-4 (Paperback)

For permission requests, speaking inquiries, and bulk order purchase options, email support@patriciabartell.com.

Interior, Cover, Layout, and Graphic Design by Corrie Nosov.

Photos by Yevgeniy Nosov.

Edited by Diamond Queen, LLC

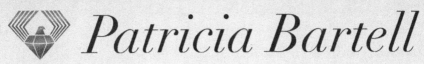

Patricia Bartell

KEYNOTE SPEAKER | PLATFORM CLOSER | WORKSHOP TRAINER

TO SCHEDULE PATRICIA TO SPEAK AT YOUR EVENT, EMAIL:

connect@patriciabartell.com

FOR MORE INFORMATION, GO TO

www.patriciabartell.com

@PATRICIABARTELLOFFICIAL

Dedication

To my mom, Deborah (Debby) Johnston

Through you, I came to understand the *true* warmth, understanding, and acceptance of a mother's heart.

You helped bring healing to my deepest wounds, standing by me when I needed it most.

Never underestimate the power of your purpose, for you've reshaped and transformed my world.

Thank you for loving and caring for me as your daughter. You fulfilled the promise that ensured I would "no longer carry the reproach of being an orphan."

ENDORSEMENTS FOR 'FROM CRUTCHES TO CRUSHING IT'

"Patricia Bartell's unflinching and triumphant tale, *From Crutches to Crushing It*, is a resounding testament to the human spirit. With profound insights and unyielding resilience, her journey from pain to power inspires us to embrace our own stories, transforming obstacles into stepping stones towards personal and professional success."

—GILBERTO REYES
HOHNER Brand Manager
Nashville, Tennessee USA

"Patricia Bartell gives us front-row seats to her transformative journey in *From Crutches to Crushing It*. Over the years that I've known her, I've seen Patricia invest hundreds of hours and multiple thousands of dollars in developing herself and her business. Throughout these pages, she demonstrates why she is a living testament to transmuting adversity into triumph. She doesn't just share her victories—she lays bare the raw, unfiltered lessons that propelled her to success. This is much more than a memoir; it's a roadmap for resilience and success."

—SHEREESE ALEXANDER
Podcast Coach and FOUNDER of Lighting Pod
Los Angeles, California USA

"This book, by Patricia Bartell, is not just another personal development book...no, no, no... it's much beyond that. It's a book that ignites the desire of success within you and not only to dream about it, but it will empower you to take the necessary steps to crush it and ultimately win in life and in business. If you're not sure whether you have what it takes, this book will definitely show you your maximum potential and help you to shine even more. Don't miss this opportunity; success is right at your doorstep - pick up the book, read it, and see you grow and shine with the actions you take."

—SUKHDEV (DEV SETHI)
Global Sales Champion 2019 and CEO
Stella Wealth, AUSTRALIA

"Patricia is a deeply inspiring soul with a story that's so relatable she can reach us where we are and give us the encouragement and reassurance we need to continue becoming the person we need to become in order to live our own dreams. Thank you, Patricia, for your authentic light! You are the burning candle that lights others' and inspires us all to shine!"

—**CYNTHIA DAY**
Co-Founder Trust Builders Network
Broker Trusted Results Realty, LLC
CEO Trusted Hospitality Group
Dallas, Texas USA

"Knowing Patricia's backstory and the person she is today, one would think these are two different people. But the story you are about to read in this book shows how any life obstacle can be overcome. Patricia's inner brightness and drive are infectious. Not to mention her passion to see anyone she comes into contact with succeed in whatever ambitions they have and to find fulfillment while achieving it. What you will take away after you read this book is a new-found power within and a belief that you can achieve anything!"

—**GARRETT FROMME**
Founder/CEO IDC Woodcraft
Madison, Indiana USA

" 'I have to show up as my authentic self, and I have to accept that not everyone will like me, and that needs to be OK.' Patricia's story is not only inspiring and compelling, but it is a beautifully crafted tapestry that illustrates her strength as a seeker of what is possible despite inconceivable obstacles and challenges. She goes deep into her personal journey and each step provides the reader with hope and wisdom readily applied to anyone who desires a life filled with joy, purpose, meaning, and intention. Her successes are laced with raw emotional moments of questioning, as we all have, and her perseverance is a testament to the resilience of the human spirit. It is a captivating account of her vision quest mission, and the takeaways are rich and plentiful!"

—**DR. JODY GRAVES**
Director of Piano Studies and Music Program Director,
Eastern Washington University
Board President - MusicFest Northwest
Spokane, Washington USA

"I met Patricia as part of a mastermind group. Wherever she was called upon, she gave her best. Looking at her life story (or should I say tale of woe), one could have expected anything else. Her journey from an unwanted child and no support to a successful entrepreneur, author, and keynote speaker is a shining example of willpower, strength, and assertiveness. Her story in *From Crutches to Crushing It* inspires, motivates, and encourages you to question 'and re-evaluate your own possibilities. The book has the potential to become a new beacon of personal motivation. I wish Patricia every success in this endeavor. She has honestly earned it."

—RALF ARMBRÜSTER
CEO and Founder of Intellicon GmbH
Blieskastel, GERMANY

"I can't say enough about Patricia Bartell's resilience and her ability to adapt to life's challenges. I'm so amazed by her story! She's also become a dear friend of mine, and I can personally say that she's truly a genuine and sincere human being. Patricia is the epitome of perseverance!"

—SELENA LÒPEZ HINOJOSA, MES
CEO- LIFT by Selina & Transformation Coach
Corpus Christi, Texas USA

"Thank you, Patricia, for being an extraordinary role model and for the difference you make in this world. *From Crutches to Crushing It* is a beacon of inspiration and resilience. Patricia transcends victimhood and embraces life, offering not just a book but a transformational journey. A must-read for those eager to overcome challenges and aspire for greatness."

—KARL ROUSSEL
Business Coach, FOUNDER of Oui c'est possible consultant INC.
(Yes, It's Possible Consultant INC.)
Edmundston, New-Brunswick CANADA

"*From Crutches to Crushing It*—telling Patricia's journey—is a great reminder that very few things in life can stop if you truly desire to succeed that the power to change and be happy indeed lies within each and every one of us. Her inspiring story in this book motivates you to take action, transforming every adversity in life into your biggest strength."

—VLAD HU
Tech Consultant and Founder at SaaS Insiders
Austin, Texas USA

"Patricia Bartell's *From Crutches to Crushing It* is not just a book; it's a masterful odyssey of resilience, transformation, and unwavering hope. As a Love and Relationship Coach who frequently engages with powerful, successful women, I recognize the importance of stories that reignite our inner spark and help us remember our worth. Patricia's journey from facing tremendous adversities to celebrating grand triumphs serves as an electrifying beacon for every woman who's ever felt lost amidst her success, longing for deeper connections within the soul. And through her journey, may you find the motivation to turn your own challenges into unparalleled victories. Highly recommended!"

—**SYLVIA SILVERS**
Love Reconnector
CEO of Sylvia Silvers Academy
Tartu, ESTONIA

"*From Crutches to Crushing It* is a game-changer for anyone ready to level up in life. Patricia Bartell delivers a masterclass in resilience and personal transformation. Forget linear paths; this is about stacking experiences to build an indomitable spirit. A must-read for IT pros, entrepreneurs, or, frankly, anyone who's dealt with setbacks and is hungry for a reboot. Embrace this journey from pain to power; you'll come out not just skilled but empowered."

—**SABRISH CHAND**
Business & IT Consultant
Founder of International Institute of IT & Consulting,
Saskatchewan, CANADA

"In a world overflowing with stories, Patricia Bartell's *From Crutches to Crushing It* is an example of inspiration and resilience. I've had the privilege of knowing Patricia for years, and her authenticity shines through every page of this book. Just as she's done for me, Patricia will guide you through an enlightening journey of determination and triumph. Don't hesitate. Dive into this extraordinary journey."

—**DEBRA KOSTIW**
Certified Master Dementia Strategist
Corporate Trainer & Speaker
Author of *Forget Me Not*
Rochester, New York USA

"I'm not overstating this one bit: meeting and becoming friends with Patricia has truly been one of the highlights of my life. It is with great pride and enthusiasm that I endorse *From Crutches to Crushing It* and Patricia for her remarkable achievements and the positive impact she has made through her business and advocacy efforts. She is a shining example of how the skills learned in self-defense with firearms class can not only enhance personal safety but also pave the way for exceptional success."

—ROB GOLDEN
When Seconds Count
Tampa, Florida USA

"Patricia Bartell's *From Crutches to Crushing It* is a beacon of hope in a world often marked by despair and adversity. Her remarkable journey, from orphan and polio survivor to a successful businesswoman and world champion, serves as a testament to the power of resilience. This book is a guide to empowerment and personal growth, offering invaluable lessons in self-confidence, transformative perspectives, and the strength found in adversity. It reminds us that we are defined not by our circumstances, but by how we respond to them. Patricia's story is an inspiration for dreamers and doers from all walks of life. It shows that every stumble and painful moment can be a stepping stone toward personal and professional success. *From Crutches to Crushing It* is a powerful narrative that will leave an indelible mark on your heart and soul."

–TERTIUS VAN EEDEN
CEO and Founder of Print on Demand
Cape Town, SOUTH AFRICA

"Patricia Bartell embodies grit and transformation. Her journey *From Crutches to Crushing It* is a vivid reminder that we're not defined by the challenges life throws at us, but by how we rise above them. This isn't just a story; it's a wake-up call to find your own power and purpose."

— NICK SANTONASTASSO
World-Renowned Keynote Speaker

"In *From Crutches to Crushing It*, Patricia Bartell navigates the intricacies of life with the grace and precision one might find in a timeless piece of art. Her narrative, woven with authenticity and depth, serves as a guiding light for all who embark on a journey of self-discovery and transformation. Just as each note in a composition carries weight, so does every experience in Patricia's journey. This is a testament to the transformative power of unwavering determination and courage."

—ECKART PREU
Music Director at Cincinnati Chamber Orchestra
Music Director at The Portland Symphony Orchestra
Music Director at Long Beach Symphony
New York, New York USA

"In *From Crutches to Crushing It*, Patricia Bartell masterfully illustrates the unyielding power of determination, resilience, and personal growth. Patricia's journey is both enlightening and empowering: offering readers actionable insights to elevate their lives—highly recommended for anyone on the path to personal and professional excellence."

—BRIAN TRACY
Global Authority on Personal Development
Chairman and CEO of Brian Tracy International

"*From Crutches to Crushing It*, written by Patricia Bartell is filled with awe inspiring stories of Patricia overcoming her challenges in life and in business. If you are struggling with your life because of various reasons, and feel as though you're not worthy of accomplishing your hopes and dreams, I recommend you to read this book immediately."

—DAN LOK
Managing Partner of DragonX Capital
Business Mentor With 10+ Million Social Media Followers

The Truth Shall Set You Free

You are not broken.

You don't need fixing.

There is nothing wrong with you!

Now, go *"Crush It"* Champion!

Contents

MOVEMENT TWO:
"CRUSHING IT" AS THE MUSICIAN

MOVEMENT THREE:
"CRUSHING IT" AS THE MUSIC EDUCATOR

MOVEMENT FOUR:
"CRUSHING IT" AS THE BUSINESS VISIONARY

THE 'CRUSH IT'

COMMUNICATION COURSE SERIES

(Total Value: $1,779)

Crush It with First Impressions *(Value: $297)*

Crush It with Unstoppable Confidence *(Value: $297)*

Crush It with Conversational Mastery *(Value: $297)*

Crush It with Leadership & Influence *(Value: $297)*

BONUS: Crush Emotional Barriers *(Value: $197)*

BONUS: Crush It by Finding Your Voice *(Value: $197)*

BONUS: Crush It with Brain Hacks to Learn Anything Faster! *(Value: $197)*

A Special Gift Just for YOU!

In appreciation for your trust and for picking up this book, I'm granting you exclusive access to this high-value course bundle. This is not just about communication; it's about transforming your internal and external influence.

Captivate. Connect. Close. Every. Single. Time.

Access at PatriciaBartell.com/Bonus

FORWARD

By Dr. Bruce Allen

In my life, I have had the privilege of meeting hundreds of individuals from many nations. On a few occasions, I have met individuals that impacted my life and stood out. Patricia Bartell is not only one of the rare few who has stood out – she has been head and shoulders above the rest!

I met Patricia as a freshly minted graduate of Whitworth University. At the time, she was teaching music as well as attending a local Bible school. On this inauspicious occasion, I was at the president of the Bible school's home visiting him and his wife with a friend of mine. Patricia had called and asked if she could come over and visit. She was curious about what a prophetic minister was like in their 'real life' aside from standing in the pulpit teaching.

I told her we were headed for the local coffee shop, and she could meet us there, to which she agreed. I don't know what she was expecting by this visit, but I do know by her reaction it wasn't exactly what she had in mind!

You see, my friend and I enjoyed bantering back and forth and making quips, keeping things light and amusing. I recall the look of surprise and wonder on her face looking back and forth between us in astonishment, shocked at our non-religious (somewhat) normal behavior. Only later, when I learned about her upbringing, did I understand her surprise and consternation! Ministers were to be pious, dignified, prim, and proper!

That original meeting over time turned into a friendship that has deepened to this day. To say that Patricia is an inspiration is sorely inadequate at best. She is a living example of a phrase I heard in my youth, 'Out of the ashes comes something beautiful.'

Her life begins with tragedy that continued into her early childhood up until she graduated from high school. Orphaned as a baby, handicapped with polio, adopted into a foreign culture, and surviving a loveless childhood were just some of the challenges she had to face and overcome.

And yet, in the crucible of these challenges, which would have crushed most, she not only endured but was fortified in her inner being and strengthened in the furnace of affliction with a resolve and tenacity that is awe-inspiring! Truly the grace of the Lord has been upon her life.

She is the living example of the Apostle Paul's statement in 2 Corinthians 7:5-6 when he said, "For indeed, when we came to Macedonia, our bodies had no rest, but were troubled on every side. Outside were conflicts, inside were fears. Nevertheless, God, who comforts the downcast, comforted us..."

In hearing her story, we watch her face each challenge with a resolve and inner strength gained through the adversity she has lived through. I have watched over the years as she has gone from one victory to another with a consistency that is almost frightening in its frequency.

And yet, if you look at the parts rather than just the whole, you will find the truth of her successes. She refuses to quit! Every seeming failure in her life has become a building block to a greater understanding of herself, her destiny, and her growth as a woman of God.

Her striving for excellence takes her out of the realm of the mediocre into the rarefied realm of the overcomer in whatever she sets her hand to.

Out of adversity comes victory to the one who does not quit, who does not concede in exhaustion, who never says 'I can't' but always 'I will!' That is Patricia.

The inspiration she has been to my wife Reshma and I, as well as the treasure she is as a sister and a friend, has been a highlight in our lives.

I'll finish with a quote from her book that encapsulates the person she is: "The mediocre teacher tells. The good teacher explains. The superior teacher demonstrates. The great teacher inspires." - William Arthur Ward

You are truly an inspiration to us! We love you, Patricia! Keep climbing the mountain of destiny set before you! You will not fail!

Dr. Bruce Allen
Still Waters International Missions

Introduction

A Note From Patricia Bartell

UNBROKEN. UNDEFEATED. UNSTOPPABLE YOU.

*L*ife can sometimes feel like a journey that takes us down an unending series of winding roads filled with potholes of despair, dead ends of failure, and precipices of pain. At times, the world around us can seem shrouded in darkness, and the crutches we lean on as if made of brittle twigs rather than solid gold. My journey began this way. I was an orphan, a polio survivor, a sufferer of abuse, a person for whom every day was a battle, an uphill struggle against odds that seemed insurmountable. But, like a phoenix rising from the ashes, I emerged victorious. Today, I am a successful businesswoman and a world champion who brings light, love, and life to those around me.

SHAPED BY CHALLENGES, NOT DEFINED BY THEM

I wrote this book because the world asked me to. Friends, family, students, colleagues, and strangers alike have all been intrigued by my story, inspired by my resilience, and eager to learn how I transformed the crutches of my past into the gold levers of my present. My life is a testament to the belief that our experiences do not define us but shape us into the people we are meant to be. In the following pages, you will find a story of inspiration and growth.

FINDING THE GIFTS HIDDEN IN THE PAIN

You will come to understand that the power to change, to be happy, and to succeed, lies within you. You will discover that you are not defined by your circumstances but by your response to them. I want you, my Champion, to find solace in my words, inspiration in my journey, and empowerment in the tools that have been instrumental in my transformation.

This book is for the dreamers, the doers, and the believers—those who are hungry for more and are willing to embrace the trials and triumphs that life presents. Whether you are a stay-at-home parent seeking self-improvement or a CEO striving for success, the lessons of this book will resonate with you. Embedded in my story are lessons about self-confidence, the power of perspective, and the magic of finding the gifts hidden in the pain.

Remember this: the beliefs we borrow from others can serve as the foundation upon which we build our self-esteem until we stand tall, unaided, and unafraid. The change we seek in the world begins with the person we see in the mirror daily. My crutches, in this tale, are so much more than mobility aids; they are a metaphor of strength, resilience, and victory. They are tokens of an epic journey from pain to power.

EMBRACE EVERY CHALLENGE

As you delve into my world, I want you to remember one thing: I wouldn't trade any part of my journey to be where I am today. Every stumble, every fall, every painful moment has shaped me into the woman I am today - strong, successful, and happy. As you turn the pages of my life, let it fuel your passion and hunger for a life of possibility.

Remember, life doesn't happen to you; it happens for you. It's not the events but our decisions that shape destiny. Every challenge, every setback, is merely a setup for a greater comeback. It's about turning those 'Crushed' moments into a life where you're not just a player, but a 'Champion'—a champion who truly 'Crushes It!' "

Welcome to my story. Experience my transformation firsthand: *From Crutches to Crushing It—A Journey from Pain to Power.*

~Patricia Bartell

COURAGE AMIDST THE SYMPHONY OF UNCERTAINTY

The pace at which a musician plays is set against the beating of the human heart.

Tempo and pulse are both measured in beats per minute. But fear makes the heart an unreliable metronome. It quickens the pulse and distorts the tick of time; the faster it beats, the faster she plays. I am no stranger to fear. I knew fear before I knew music.

It is 2015. I'm thirty-seven years old, and I'm standing in the wings of Spokane's Fox Theatre. The interior is all art deco sunbursts, enamel inlay, lacquer finishes, brass fixtures, vermillion, teal, rose pink, ivory, and onyx toned in the golden glow of soft lighting. The concert hall buzzes with the excited chatter of people taking their seats and the cacophony of orchestral instruments warming up.

I wear a long blue sequined gown to match the grandeur of the occasion. I reach for my phone, strategically placed in a pocket in one of the pouches attached to my crutches. As I do so, a button responsible for holding my dress in place comes loose. I am within one or two minutes of stepping onto the stage. Someone rushes to fasten the errant button for me. The conductor, Eckart Preu, is standing next to me. He says something, but I do not hear him. All my focus is on fear. I know this fear, and I know what to do with it: I must reverse engineer my way to calm. I must slow my heartbeat. I use the metronome on my phone. I breathe deeply and diaphragmatically. I listen closely. I clock 138 BPM. I lock it in. I'm good.

I repeat the phrase that has become my mantra, "I was made for this!" My heart fills with gratitude for the privilege of performing, for the opportunity to connect with my audience. I have learned that fear and gratitude cannot coexist. I am ready to walk confidently out onto the stage and do what I was born to do ... to share my message through music.

Eckart and I walk out together on a path flanked by the concert maestro and violinists to our right and the rest of the musicians to our left. I swing my crutches forward. The orchestra stands up. I'm mentally preparing. It's a twenty-minute program in three movements. I find my markers. I know where my teacher is sitting. I know where my friends are. I know where my students are. I cannot see them, but their catcalls and whistles reach me across the crowd. I hear my name: Patricia Bartell, guest artist with the Spokane Symphony Orchestra.

I acknowledge the audience, shake hands with Eckart, and take my seat on an elevated platform, left of center stage. The sound technician hands me my accordion and straps it firmly to my body. To coordinate and control the bellows, the buttons, and the keyboard, my accordion must become a living, breathing extension of myself. The position of a shoulder, the elevation of an elbow, the tilt of a chin, even the lift of an eyebrow, the smallest of physical nuances, will alter how the music is expressed as I play. My legs can't dance, but my body and the accordion must move to the music.

While I get strapped in, Eckart explains the score to the audience. Astor Piazzolla composed his concerto on a commission from the Banco de la Provincia de Buenos Aires in 1979. It was named *Aconcagua*, posthumously, after the highest mountain in the Americas because it was said to represent both the peak of Astor's oeuvre and because it conveys the climb to the roof of the earth, in all its facets and symbolism: pain, longing, loneliness, freedom, transfiguration, and peace.

This moment right here is my own Aconcagua. My own hard,

and far from straight, ascent.

Eckart turns to face the symphony. He raises his baton. You can hear a pin drop. I must come in with the orchestra on the very first beat. I've had only one full rehearsal and one dress rehearsal. In both, I came in a split second before the orchestra. I cannot afford to make that mistake now. This brings up a new level of nerves. I recalculate and recalibrate. I will my heart to stay steady.

It helps to know that among the musicians behind me are my friends and many of my professors from Whitworth University: my conducting instructor, Richard Strauch, my percussion instructor, Paul Raymond, and my violin instructor, Jeri Bentley. They, too, have been waiting for me to join them on the symphony's stage.

The conductor's baton goes down.

I make the beat, and as soon as we start, everything aligns.

The second movement is slower, more melodic, less tango, and less edge than the first. I play solo for eight bars. For forty seconds, it's just the accordion in a way the audience has never heard it before. Not folk, not polka, not waltz, just pure poetry. And as I finish the first small section, the lead violinist comes in, and then the piano, and then, seemingly out of nowhere, the cellos and other string instruments. The sound becomes lush and regal. I have mentally rehearsed this moment a hundred times, but now I am inside it. The music carries me. I feel its awe and its power.

The third movement is more energetic. I'm on the home stretch. I know this section well; it's easier and more playful. Now I can engage the audience, charm them, and meet them in the music.

Suddenly, without warning, I 'drop out.' The music softens.

And then the orchestra, and the audience, begin climbing, climbing, climbing as if scaling a huge mountain. It's beautiful, it's biblical, and it's very, very personal.

I play four chords repeatedly; then the strings enter, then the cello and the drums. The timpani roll in crescendo. It's building, building, building; we're reaching the very top.

And then the audience is on its feet.

"Encore! Encore!"

Two curtain calls later, I go out alone and play a solo piece, *Tango pour Claude*.

I am at the Cumbre del Aconcagua, at the summit of my own mountain.

Eight years, an international reputation, a thriving Music Academy, a six-figure business, several keynote addresses,

TEDx speeches, and a coaching career later, the fear is back. It, too, has evolved. Now, it comes by stealth at night when I'm sleeping. When my gold crutches are resting against the wall. It catches me off guard, grips my heart, and sets the metronome ticking at a terrifying pace. 'Boom de boom, boom de boom,' triple time. It catches me defenseless. No markers. No reverse engineering. I feel like I'm disappearing. Discombobulating. Death by exploding heart. I reach for something tangible. This is my face; these are my arms; this is my bed. I pray to God. I pray out loud: "Heavenly Father, help." This is my voice. These are my eyes. I force them open... I'm back.

The fear lingers for a few minutes and then slips away like a soundless assassin who realizes he must finish the job another day. Fear wears black and carries a loaded weapon, but I know it well. I know where it comes from. I know why it's here. I could identify it in a line-up. I have come a long way, swinging my crutches one before the other. But if I'm to go further still, I need to become Rogue Killer to this last-standing sharpshooter who waits between me and infinite possibility.

I must raise my voice.

I must tell my story.

Movement One

"CRUSHING IT" WITH RESILIENCE

"In the midst of winter, I found there was, within me, an invincible summer. And that makes me happy. For it says that no matter how hard the world pushes against me, within me, there's something stronger—something better, pushing right back."

—Albert Camus

One

AGAINST ALL ODDS

*"The weight of our beginnings does
not determine the height of our future."*
—*Patricia Bartell*

At four-and-a-half years old, I was born for a second time in Terminal C at Spokane International Airport, Washington State. Brought in from Bolivia without an umbilical cord, I was coaxed through the landing bridge, clinging to my adopted father, Gordon Bartell.

The Bartells had chosen me from a worldwide catalog of orphans published in a magazine called 'OURS.' The title seems significant. Because we belonged to nobody, we belonged to everybody or anybody. Each disenfranchised child was listed by name, photograph, and a short description. I stood out as the only child with no picture and no paragraph. Even my name was circumspect. I was indexed as Patricia Mamani, but as I would eventually discover, Mamani is to Bolivia what Smith is to America. I was the Jane Doe of orphans.

GOLD NUGGET

We are more than the categories others assign.
Define your narrative and embrace its power.

In the absence of a documented history or reliable account, all I know about my earliest years is what is written on my body: An illegible scar wrapping around my left ankle and another tracking down behind my right ear, both suggesting abuse or at least neglect. For the longest time, I believed that my atrophied legs and lame feet, caused by infant polio, were why I often felt so rejected. They are certainly why I never could walk.

There is no one more invisible or with less agency than a parentless girl of color from a third-world country, except maybe this: an orphan with polio. Statistically, I had almost zero chance of surviving infancy. When I did, the doctors did not believe I'd reach age seven. And even if I inexplicably made it that far, at fourteen, if not adopted, I would be turned onto the streets of La Paz where, as a cripple, my chances of survival would be none. Whatever the circumstances surrounding my origin, this is certain: I was sentenced to death many times before I knew my name.

GOLD NUGGET

In life, the weight of others' expectations can be heavier than any physical burden. When we shed that weight, it's often the key to finding our true selves and true freedom.

In 1983 Gordon Bartell flew from the USA to Bolivia to collect me. He found me dirty, malnourished, and undersized, crawling on the orphanage's stony dusty floor. He was confused. When he asked the nuns, who ran the orphanage, in broken Spanish: "Why she not walk?" They answered, in broken English: "She walk, but sometime she choose not to."

Gordon took one look at my tiny feet and said to himself, "This child has never walked." His decision to take me anyway, despite the opaque advertising, was an act of mercy and a miracle and the reason I'm here today.

He would have quickly realized the burden of responsibility—the doctors he'd have to pay, the medications and crutches he would have to buy. But instead of measuring the cost, he saw only opportunity. He was my one chance of survival. He would make me his daughter and give me the gift of life. And for that, I carry on his last name and continue his legacy.

The Bartells turned out in numbers at the arrival lounge to greet me. Gordon and Barbara had six grown-up biological children and two adopted children, Native Indian American boys Kenny and James, three and two years older than me, respectively. Unable to speak the language, overwhelmed by the sea of foreign-looking faces, distrusting of women, and afraid of losing my new father, I cried when Gordon tried to hand me to Barbara. And in that one act of defiance, I brought down the judge's anvil. Many years later, Barbara would tell me coldly, "You rejected me. So, I rejected you." My death sentence had been commuted to thirteen years of cruelty, confusion, and withheld love.

Emotions trigger reactions. While feelings are innate, responses are choices. Harness them.

ROOTLESS

Every morning, the snow-capped peaks of the Rocky Mountains stand clear against the blue sky. Every afternoon, storm winds streak that same sky white, and every night, lightning runs magnificent and terrible from the horizon. There are elk in the draws, American bison on the range, and above, golden eagles with seven-meter wing spans acting out a complex precision dance of predator and prey.

The landscape, partitioned into vast expanses of hay, wheat, and barley fields, is peopled with what seems to be picture-perfect barns and farmhouses from an aerial view.

This is the Flathead Valley, and the town is Charlo: 70 miles north of Missoula, 190 miles east of Spokane, and 5,500 miles from La Paz, Bolivia. This is where I live.

"Blink, and you'll miss it" is the running joke among locals. Charlo has no traffic lights or stop signs, just a green post office, a school, a bar, and a grocery store. The town is less than two square miles and has less than 400 inhabitants. The Bartells live on an eighty-acre farm with hay fields, tractors, balers, and barns. There's a large pond, an enormous garden, several milk cows, a small herd of cattle, some pigs, chickens, nine dogs, twelve cats, and eighteen children.

Most of the biological Bartell kids have already left home or are in the process of marrying and moving on by the time I arrive. I am the third adopted child and the first adopted girl. Over the next thirteen years, nine more orphans will arrive. Cameron and Nicole came from Mexico. We call them 'the family twins.' Even though they have different parents, they are only one day apart and only weeks old when we get them. Then Sunny, Ben, and Amy from Brazil. They are older, about nine, seven, and five years old. They all have the same mother but different fathers, and they all have fetal alcohol syndrome. Next is Shawn. Shawn is fostered, not adopted, and he doesn't stay long. Then follows John, Daniel, and finally, Seth, all three blond-haired, blue-eyed Caucasian Americans.

All I'm ever told about my own beginnings is that I was 'unwanted' and that my parents were probably in prison. I never dared ask more. And I assume it's the same for the others.

We grow like moss, tenuously, on the dark, damp bark of

another's family tree.

Our home is a sprawling two-story house with two steps leading to a wide veranda lined with muddy work boots. The entrance leads directly into a large kitchen with patterned green linoleum floors that clash with the yellow Formica countertops. There are thirteen steps, carpeted with burnt-red commercial floor covering, leading to the upstairs bedrooms, where I sleep.

I know these details well. I count the steps every time I hoist myself up them, slowly, one by one. I have an intimate relationship with the floor. In the absence of workable feet, I crawl everywhere. Outside, I have a royal blue metal makeshift wheely with handlebars and a simple seat rigged between two thick tires, which I spin against the grass, hay, gravel, snow, and mud.

Until I learned to use crutches at the age of ten, my main chore was, inevitably, to scrub the floors. Chores regulate our lives. "Idle hands are the devil's workshop," Barbara says. We work all day, starting before sunrise. We milk the cows, strain the milk, sew, do the laundry, prepare the food, weed the garden, work in fields, wash the floors ... the list of chores is endless. This is farm life. The Devil will find no vacancy here.

GEMS OF WISDOM FOR CHAMPIONS

We've all been that outsider or were placed in an entirely unfamiliar situation. But in those chilling silences, I unearthed my resilience. Every time you feel alone, remember: Champions see it as an invitation to discover depths within yet to be explored.

There was a time when I saw certain parts of my life as blemishes. But here's the twist: our perceived disadvantages often forge our most formidable strengths. Ask yourself: What if the very challenge I face today is sculpting my tomorrow's strength?

There was a time when I saw certain parts of my life as blemishes. But here's the twist: our perceived disadvantages often forge our most formidable strengths. Ask yourself: What if the very challenge I face today is sculpting my tomorrow's strength?

When life handed me a second chance, it wasn't just another chance; it was a profound reminder that hope renews and every sunrise brings a new story. Embrace those second chances. They're life whispering, "You've got this, and the best is yet to come."

Two

THE NINTH STEP

"The heaviest burdens we carry are the emotions
we don't express. Acknowledge them and
let them pass through you."
—Patricia Bartell

*G*ordon Bartell is a kind man of few words. He is a
long-haul truck driver and owns five heavy-duty vehicles
crisscrossing the Pacific Northwest. He spends months in
solitude, alone with his thoughts on the open road. When he
does come home, two weeks here, a week there, he spends all
day in the open fields or working in the sheds and then likes
to come back to the house and sit in his chair in silence. He
doesn't much like noise, so we work quietly around him. Still,
he is the one who wakes up earliest to put logs on the stove to
warm the house. He is the one who wakes us children up in the

morning with an affectionate rub of his grizzly beard and who looks in on us at night. I love him and call him Daddy.

I never observe even the smallest gesture of affection between Daddy and Barbara. I know they drink dark, bitter Yuban coffee together in the dimly lit living room in the early hours before day breaks. I suspect their conversations are practical, dry, and sparse—mostly about what needs to be done that day.

Barbara is a plain, stocky, gray-haired woman, humorless and stoic. She believes in the rule of law and never drives her big red van over the posted speed limit. When not pulling weeds in the garden, she sits, reading, in her rocking chair in the living room. I watch other mothers with their children on our monthly shopping trips to Costco in Missoula. They are young, stylish, and beautiful. They smile when their children talk. They are laughing and playful and seem to be having fun with their kids. They drive Subaru station wagons. They represent everything I feel I do not have.

Over the next few chapters, you will read about some of my experiences with Barbara but understand that there was a major gift in all this and that she played a major role in who I am today. Although I don't endorse many of her methods, I know she believed she did the best she knew with the resources she had. I would go through all these experiences again to have what I have today. This is true healing, the kind that comes through acceptance, forgiveness, and choice.

Barbara does not often engage in idle chit-chat. She is direct and to the point. She does not do hugs, hair strokes, Band-Aids, or small talk.

She is God-fearing and follows the Bible to the letter of the word. Hers is a literal, righteous, and punishing God. 'Children should be seen and not heard' is her second favorite biblical quote. Her first is, 'Spare the rod; spoil the child.' And if there was one thing Barbara did not do, it was spoil the children.

Her rod is sometimes a horsewhip, the back of a brush, a wire hanger, or a willow branch. For a woman who does not promote metaphor, Barbara's interpretation of 'the rod' is surprisingly loose. But the wounds are painful, and the bruises linger for days.

There is no way to anticipate and, therefore, avert a beating from Barbara. Truly, I get beaten for scuffing the knees of my new white Easter tights, even though I crawl because I cannot walk. I am beaten for 'messing' with the muskrats. Kenny and James have told me that if you clap your hands in a certain way, the sound magically draws the amphibious rodents from the bottom of the farm pond. It worked, but to this day, I do not understand why we got beaten for that one. I get in trouble for speaking or laughing too loudly, gesturing too dramatically, or drawing attention to myself.

The beatings are almost always for something trivial—

forgetting to wash a dish, leaving a light on, or speaking out of turn. And the punishment is always disproportionate to the crime. Only once, during a particularly brutal beating, do I try to talk back: "You never beat the boys this hard," I challenge. Barbara doubles down. I never defy her again.

Sometimes, I hear Barbara ascend the stairs to our bedrooms. The staircase creaks as she climbs, like the crescendo in a horror movie. I hold my breath, frozen with fear. Is my bed creased? Is the trash empty? Are my clothes folded? Barbara might pick up a piece of paper, a toy, or some clothes left on the floor and throw it in the trash on her way out. Or the inoffensive item can become a live grenade, triggering a tirade. There is just no way of knowing. And I live in fear of what might happen or what mistake I might make.

Gold Nugget

There are two sides to fear. One is when you are in physical danger and the other is made up.

Because of Barbra's unpredictability, we live in a perpetual, unnatural, heightened state of fight or flight. She rules by fear and uncertainty, and as a result, we are the best-behaved kids in Charlo.

I also experienced other forms of punishment: affectional neglect, isolation, and humiliation. We're unceremoniously dismissed from the dinner table without supper, given additional chores, or made ashamed of our changing bodies. The worst is the 'cold shoulder.' When I get into trouble, Barbara and the others walk past me like I don't exist. I would be treated as if invisible for hours, even days. "If mama ain't happy; ain't nobody happy" are words I often hear as I move ghost-like through the farm. At these times, I feel I'm worth less than an old piece of furniture, just another unacknowledged object or a mistake to be erased.

The first time I experienced heartache as a real, terrible, pressing pain in my chest, I was seven or eight years old. Barbara exiled me from the living room, for I know not what. In a rare hour of entertainment, the family is watching The Lone Ranger, and I can hear the muted soundtrack as I crawl up those thirteen steps to my room.

Step one, step two: What is ... wrong with me?

Step three, step four: My chest ... hurts.

Step five, step six: My heart ... is sore.

Step seven, step eight: Can a heart ... explode?

By step nine, I can go no further. I curl up in a ball and do not know if I am dying, disappearing, or just falling asleep. The pain is almost unbearable.

And there I lie for the longest time. Eventually, I crawl up the remaining steps and into my bedroom. There is no one to sweep me off the floor.

Christmas is a big deal in the Bartell home. We spend days prepping. We are poor, so usually, we kids share everything. For example, we're expected to peel off segments for our siblings if we're given an orange. It feels like giving a kidney. But for Christmas, we each get our own orange. The real highlight of Christmas day, though, is the family recital. Everyone gathers in the living room and gets to perform a piece of music, a poem, or a song. My older sisters, Callie, Phyllis, and Sarah, sing, "I'll be home for Christmas." It's a beautiful harmony, and everyone applauds. Then it's my turn.

I've been practicing for days. I crawl to the center of the room and start singing: *"There's a little white duck, sitting in the water. A little white duck, doing what he oughter..."*

I look around, nobody is smiling, and I wonder what I've done wrong. I somehow get through the song, trailing off at the end, *"...there's nobody left sitting in the water. Boo. Boo. Boo."*

The room is silent. No applause. I crawl back to my place. My chest hurts.

Barbara insists that we call her Mama. Not mom or mommy but Mama. I suspect a bridge exists between where I am and where she wants me to be. If I could cross it, I could reach her. But I don't know how. I try. My brothers and I are sitting on the living room floor. Barbara is in her rocker. One of my brothers suddenly looks up at her and says, "I love you, Mama." Barbara returns the look and says, "Oh, that's sweet." It's the best she can offer; 'love' is not in her lexicon. I think to myself, "Hmm. I'll try that." "I love you too, Mama," I say. She shifts her gaze to me and answers, "I don't believe you." My chest hurts.

Barbara does not know how to cross that bridge either. She calls me to sit alongside her on the couch and shows me a photo. It's an image of me sitting on a ledge and staring into the camera lens. "Look," she says, "look at your face; look at your eyes." 'Resentful' is a word she uses. 'Ungrateful' is another. These are sins, according to her Good Book. She launches into an abstract philosophical monologue on gratitude and goodness. I don't understand what she is saying. And I don't know what to answer. I am empty, voiceless. When I look at the picture, all I see is a very sad girl who just wants to be loved. My chest hurts.

GEMS OF WISDOM FOR CHAMPIONS

I frequently mention the physical pain in my chest when confronted with emotional pain. Life has a poignant way of merging our emotional and physical worlds. When your heart bears the weight of emotions, ask: "What thought is triggering this emotion?"

There were moments when I felt voiceless or powerless. But here's the magic: our power isn't lost; it's waiting to be reclaimed. Each time you feel voiceless, remember that your voice is just a whisper away, waiting for you to amplify it.

I've danced the dance of seeking approval, shifting and molding myself to fit another's vision. Yet, the most transformative question I've ever asked is: "Am I being true to myself?" Today, my Champion, challenge yourself: Are the roles you're playing truly in harmony with who you really are? Who did you have to become to get the validation you were seeking, and is it serving you today?

Free Bonus Training: "Crush Emotional Barriers"

Access at PatriciaBartell.com/bonus

Three

"WHAT IS WRONG WITH ME?"

"There're no limits to what you can do when you understand how *you learn best."*
—Patricia Bartell

My schooling is delayed by a year until I am seven to give me more time to become proficient in English. We are homeschooled, or more accurately, we sit at the kitchen table and teach ourselves from textbooks. Even so, I look forward to starting. I want to be smart and a good student so I can win Barbara's approval and the respect of my siblings. And I am eager to learn. But I soon discover that learning doesn't come easy to me.

51

The first challenge is basic phonetic English, which consists of knowing what sounds the letters stand for and how to blend those sounds into words. I stare at the phonetic symbols, feeling completely lost. They look like nonsense squiggles and dots, and I simply can't figure out how they relate to the sounds I'm supposed to make. It's like trying to decipher a secret code. I wonder: "What is wrong with me?"

I never feel as if I'm being taught; I feel as if I'm trying to follow marching orders. Of course, I know now that it takes a human voice to infuse words with shades of deeper meaning. Most children cannot learn from flat black ink on an impersonal page.

I am quizzed on spelling and pronunciation; when I get it wrong, I must write the words out tens, sometimes hundreds of times. I have composition books filled with lines and lines of repeated words. It's a tedious and frustrating process that makes my wrists ache.

As for math, it's a magic language only a few can understand. I'm not one of them. We use the Saxon arithmetic system, where each lesson builds on the next. I fall exponentially further behind until it feels like I'm trying to push my way up a down-moving escalator. I spend hours working through a single problem, only to realize that I've missed a crucial step and have to start from the beginning again. I am drowning in a sea of numbers and symbols. I wonder: "What is wrong with me?

My feelings of failure are compounded by the horrors of history, which I'm expected to regurgitate by rote. To make matters worse, James is whip-smart when it comes to memorizing. He can recite passages from books, and rattle off the names of historical figures and events with ease, while I struggle to remember even the most basic facts. "What is wrong with me?" I ask myself. "What is wrong with my mind?"

It is only years later, when I become a teacher, that I realize how different minds work in different ways; that the problem was never a lack of intelligence but rather the result of a system that had failed me.

THE ACCORDION PLAYER

Every child in the Bartell household is mandated to play a musical instrument. Little did I know that this would be my lifeline. And because the only available instrument is the upright piano in the living room, we can either sing or play piano. Except for James, he gets to play the accordion. I idolize my brother. He is cool. And if James plays the accordion, that's cool, too.

But the main reason I want to play the accordion is Myron Floren. Occasionally, on Saturday afternoons at 3:00 pm, I'm allowed to watch one-hour reruns of The Lawrence Welk Show. It's a light-hearted revue popular with middle Americans for its wholesome, family-friendly style, featuring clean-cut performers playing music that's easy to dance to. The accordion is a key instrument in the Lawrence Welk sound. And Myron Floren is the king of the accordion. The man can play like nobody's business. He can play anything, from polkas to ballads, his fingers flying over the keys in lightning-fast runs and dazzling arpeggios. He wears bright suits and a smile as wide as the Flathead River, and the sound of his accordion is pure joy. Watching him on The Lawrence Welk Show is the highlight of my week. I know that I want to play the accordion, and I want to play it like Myron Floren.

What I'm really chasing, of course, is his smile, his showmanship, his joy. What I really want is his happiness. If I can play 'happy,' perhaps I can be happy.

I beg Barbara for months to allow me to play the accordion. For 6 months, she insists that I play piano instead. And then, surprisingly, she gives in. She gets me an accordion and enrolls James and me in lessons with a teacher in Missoula, Ruth Gilfillan.

Ruth is a diminutive, spritely woman in her eighties with brown dyed curly hair, and what she lacks in technical know-how, she makes up for in joviality. She can only ever teach us the basics, varying the rhythm and adding a little swing. "Oom-pah, oom-pah," she starts, then, "hop hop, one-two," she bangs her tiny fist on her thigh, bounces, and shouts, "Keep the beat, keep the beat, let's have some fun!"

Ruth is sweet and bouncy, but the accordion is more than 'fun' to me; it's a companion, a friend to my loneliness, a way out of despair. When I play the accordion, I'm not fearful, and I'm not asking, 'What's wrong with me?' I know my arms are strong, and my fingers are nimble and fast. The notes give me the words to a language I don't have; the music expresses emotions I cannot articulate.

I try to wake up extra early to finish my homework before my chores to have time to practice in the afternoon. I even try to shirk my first chore of the day, milking the cows. When Gordon comes to wake me up, I sit up and say, "Daddy, I don't think I want to milk the cows anymore." Without missing a beat, he says, "If you ever want to play like Myron Floren, you get out there and exercise those hands." I never complained about milking cows again.

While Gordon uses the accordion to motivate me, my love for music and my enthusiasm for practice offer an easier way to punish me, too. Instead of a beating, I'm told, "No accordion for you today." It hurts just as much.

GEMS OF WISDOM
FOR CHAMPIONS

Facing a steep learning curve of unknowns, I realized that every new skill starts with a small step of understanding. Remember this: Every challenge is an opportunity to discover another aspect of your potential. You only need to know the very next step in front of you to get started.

There were times when shadows of doubt clouded my vision, causing me to question my own abilities or intelligence. In those critical moments, I posed a powerful question to myself: "What if my biggest breakthrough is just beyond this?" Let this question light your way during your darkest hours. What is the question you ask internally during moments of tension or frustration? And how can you change it so it empowers you?

In the classroom of life, various teaching styles cross our path, but it was always the ones where I connected with the teacher that made a lasting mark. Their style, passion, and ability communicated in the way my brain processed the information. Dive deep: Which teachings do you remember most and why?

**Free Bonus Training: "Crush It with Brain Hacks to
Learn Anything Faster!"**

Access at PatriciaBartell.com/bonus

Four

A BETRAYAL
OF TRUST

*"Life's harshest moments teach us our strengths,
often revealing paths we never knew existed."*
—Patricia Bartell

At eight years old, I join the Brownies. They have a clubhouse in Charlo. After the white-tight-scuffed-knee Easter beating, I know better than to dirty my stockings. So, I bear crawl into the scout hall. All the neat beige uniformed little Brownies are sitting cross-legged in a semi-circle in the hall's center. They gawk wide-eyed and fascinated as I enter, the way drivers reflexively stare at roadkill. It's not so much shock they register as it is an uncomfortable curiosity. They simply don't know what to make of me. For the first time, I see myself from the outside in and wonder, "Do I look funny to them?"

It doesn't matter because my career as a bear-crawling Brownie is cut short due to complications from polio and scoliosis that are causing my hips to dislocate. At nine years old, in 1987, I undergo surgery with Doctor Johnson in Missoula that leaves me in a spica cast for several weeks. I'm put in a makeshift bed in the living room, and there I remain, propped up, in a cast from the ribs down, legs akimbo, immobilized.

The operation fails, and I'm eventually taken to Shriners Children's Hospital in Spokane, where it's explained to me that a metal rod will be attached to my right hip bone and bolted to the socket.

Despite the obvious gravity of the surgery, Shriners provides a sunny oasis in a childhood that offers little in the way of light and laughter. For the first time, my inherently extroverted nature is allowed to shine, and I blossom under the care and compassion of the hospital staff. I race up and down the corridors in a wheelchair doing wheelies, making friends with all the children, doctors, and nurses in my ward.

I become particularly attached to two nurses, Nancy McDuff, a kind middle-aged friendly woman I follow like an adoring puppy on her rounds. I see more of the human anatomy during her scrub-downs, temperature checks, and catheter changes than a nine-year-old should, but I don't care. Nancy is kind, and I'm happy to be beside her. But Nurse Kim is the one I adore. She looks like Julie Andrews, young, shy, beautiful, everything I imagined a mom would be. When my anesthetic wears off prematurely before the end of a minor surgical procedure, it's Kim that I call for. And miraculously, she comes. "It's OK," she soothes, "Everything will be alright. Go back to sleep. They're finishing up now, and you'll be just fine. Sleep now." And I sleep.

But everything is not alright because one day, in walks Neilanne Cooper. Neilanne Cooper with a long body, long salt and pepper hair, a long nose, and librarian spectacles. Neilanne Cooper with the fake smile and the hidden agenda. The nurses say, "There's someone here we'd like you to meet. She's a friend." And I think, "Oh good, another friend."

Neilanne Cooper has a way of asking questions, which I realize, too late, is how social workers are trained to interrogate children. "And what did they do?" ... "Oh really? And why do you think they did that?" ... "Tell me..." Any discomfort I feel is overridden by the fact that this woman seems genuinely interested in what I, Patricia Bartell, have to say. And I say it all. Of course, I don't know that how we are disciplined at home is unacceptable. I don't know differently. I'm just happy to talk about farm life and have someone listen. So, by the time Neilanne Cooper drops the friendly façade, it's way too late. The bomb's ticking, and there is no way to diffuse it.

By all calculations, I should have been at Shriners for about four months. The operation is serious, and the recovery is slow. I need to be in another spica cast for six more weeks, fitted with orthopedic braces and taught to use crutches. The braces run the lengths of my legs, from thigh to ankle. They have clunky metal release clips, two on each side of the knee, for when I sit down. The clips take time to lock and unlock, and they do so with a loud cable-snapping sound that will mortify me later as a self-conscious teenager. I will eventually stop wearing the right-leg brace because my right leg is stronger than the left. And in my twenties, engineering upgrades will result in braces with a single, simple, soundless clip that I can slide up and down with a magician's sleight of hand.

For now, though, I need both braces to maintain stability.

Walking on crutches is difficult for any injured person; for someone who has never walked, it's a challenge that requires the help of an experienced team of doctors and physiotherapists trained in orthopedics, encouragement, and kindness.

I need balance to stay upright, momentum to propel myself forward, core strength to push down and swing, and coordination to maintain my gait. Fortunately, I'm a fast learner. In a few weeks, I go from trembling like a newborn deer to climbing stairs, navigating crowded spaces, and spinning around.

Gold Nugget

In the face of adversity, the human spirit's resilience shines brightest, turning stumbling blocks into stepping stones.

But four months at Shriners becomes five and then six. And during that time, I've had only one visitor.

My dad, on a cross-country drive, has made a detour through Spokane to visit me. Other than that, I've had no guests or phone calls, which has raised a red flag. The staff has contacted Child Protection Services, who have dispatched Neilanne Cooper.

Gold Nugget

No matter how vast the darkness, there's always a light, even if it's just a glimmer, beckoning us to find our way.

Neilanne Cooper drops the bomb: I will not return to the farm; I'll go to a foster family. A file has been opened on Barbara and Gordon to investigate possible abuse. Now I know something is very wrong, that I've done something very wrong.

And all I can think is, "I'm going to get the worst beating of my life for this."

GEMS OF WISDOM FOR CHAMPIONS

There was a moment, a fleeting instant, when I glimpsed myself through another's eyes. The revelation was profound. It wasn't about validation but understanding. Today, I ask: are we truly seeing ourselves, or merely reflections shaped by perceptions?

From life's tapestry, an unexpected thread wove its way to me, becoming an anchor. Their qualities? They mirrored the depth and richness inside me. Remember: Like attracts like. If you are drawn to certain qualities in another person, they are also in you.

Trust, so swiftly granted, can fracture in the blink of an eye. I've felt that break, and it's reshaped the contours of my heart. Yet, in the aftermath, I challenge myself: Will I let one moment define all others, or will I bravely build anew?

Five

THE STRUGGLE TO BELONG AGAIN

*"The shadows of our past can either ensnare us
or propel us towards growth."*
—Patricia Bartell

*M*y foster parents are a regular, nice-enough, childless couple. Ron, a policeman, is a friendly, what-you-see-is-what-you-get kind of guy. Donna is a thickset housewife. With her, everything is always 'happy, happy, happy,' and I don't trust her at all. Coming out of my room one evening, I stand in the passageway, eavesdropping while they discuss me. Donna calls me a sullen, unsure, on-off little girl, and after that, I keep her at arms-length. I try to be polite and sweet, but I am confused and lonely. I've always been surrounded by other children, and being alone feels foreign. But mostly, I'm just full of fear.

I remember my stay with Ron and Donna as one does a nightmare; the sounds are muted, the images are vague, and the memories slip through my fingers as I try to retrieve them. All that is left is the terror. Terror of the chaos I've unleashed on the Bartells, terror of what will happen to them, to me. Terror of the punishment that I am certain awaits me. Nobody tells me anything. I don't know what the future holds. I'm like a death row inmate counting down to my last rite of passage, except I have no idea when that might be or if I'll be put down by noose or lethal injection.

Terror draws a blank. I might have been with Ron and Donna for two months, maybe three or even four. It might have been summer because I didn't go to school. I must have eaten meals with them, but I don't remember. They probably took me out sometimes, I don't remember. Stress, panic, loneliness, exile, that's what I remember.

Barbara, wanting to show me what a terrible thing I had done and what I'd put the children through, would later paint this picture: Everyone was home, minding their own business, when Neilanne Cooper swooped in, accompanied by an armed CPS officer. She interrogated Barbara (Gordon was away on the truck), then spoke to each child individually and asked them to raise their shirts so she could check for marks, scars, and bruises. The kids, under Barbara's mandate, clammed up. Neilanne Cooper, invested with a little power, became way too pushy and seemingly oblivious to the epic destruction she'd wreaked on my world.

Now and then, someone comes to Ron and Dawn's house to ask me questions: "Is this how it happened... Like this? ... Like that?" I see that the investigation is not going anywhere; things are getting worse. I never retract my accounts or claim to have made it up; I just quit talking. My responses are laconic: "It's not that bad. It's fine. I want to go home.

The entire episode is a debacle, and in the absence of incriminating evidence, Neilanne Cooper is banned from the farm, the inquiry is closed, and a decision is made to return me to the Bartells. I've been gone for more than nine months.

I walk up the two steps to the wide porch and enter through the open front door. There is nobody to greet me. I don't know what to do, where to go, or where to put my little suitcase. So, I sit awkwardly, shamefully, on a chair at the entrance and wait, and wait, and wait. My siblings walk past without greeting me. I am heartbroken and scared. I still don't know what my punishment will be.

At last, Barbara comes. Without looking at me, she tells me to take my things upstairs and hands me a list of chores. My chest hurts.

For weeks, nobody speaks to me. My brothers only know the story they've been told and are understandably angry with me, the 'difficult one' who has caused so much turmoil for the family. I am the black sheep of the family now. The younger and newer ones barely remember me and don't know how to behave around me. I've been gone a long time, and I'm an unfamiliar, unwelcome presence, the 'bad girl' who brought horrible people into their lives and disrupted the certainty of their routine. So, I do the only things I can: I throw myself into my chores; I buckle down and work; I learn to bury my pain in labor. An incredible work ethic is another unintended but extremely valuable consequence of this terrible time, a gift that will prove to be priceless.

Gold Nugget

An incredible work ethic is another unintended but extremely valuable consequence of this terrible time, a gift that will prove to be priceless.

To be fair, there is never much time to talk on the farm anyway. There's way too much to do. Aside from domestic work, there's plowing, disking, and harrowing in the fall, bucking and baling in the spring. There are animals to feed, earth to irrigate, a giant garden to weed, and tractors to run.

By the end of our chores, we're usually smudged with dirt and sweat, our clothes caked with hay and dust. We march onto the porch, boots clomping heavily, stomachs growling with hunger, faces red, and hands calloused.

We eat together at the large dining room table, soup or stew with meat from the farm animals, greens, and potatoes from the garden. Nobody speaks much. We scrape our plates with spoons or forks, the clatter of utensils often being the only conversation. At the end of the meal, we all sit, tired and silent, our hands folded in our laps, waiting to be excused.

Now that I use crutches, I teach myself to drive the green John Deere tractor, using my crutches to push down and release the breaks. First, a circular swather must cut the hay and lay it in windrows. Then, a tedder is attached to the tractor and driven over the hay, lifting, turning, and spreading it, row by row, so that all sides are exposed to the sun. Finally, the dried hay must be raked into larger piles that are easier to buck and bale. It's painfully slow, repetitive work, steering the tractor up and down inch by inch, over and over the same tracks for hours and hours.

After a particularly long hot day, I return to the house with red, burning, scratchy eyes that feel as if they've been sand-papered and watering tear ducts. I can barely see. The reflection of the sun bouncing off the polished surface of the tractor, exacerbated by the glare of the hay, has burnt my eyes. Photokeratitis it's called, and it's very, very painful.

As the weeks go on, I commit to my chores. I am fast but thorough. For any new tasks, I quickly find the most efficient way to get them done. I never complain. I just do. And do. And do.

I overhear Barbara telling my brothers, "Well, at least she knows how to work." It's the closest I've come in weeks to an acknowledgment of my existence. But it tattoos onto my psyche an unhealthy connection between excessive work and acceptance that will take a lifetime to abrade.

Another time, I am alone in my bedroom, looking out the window, watching the bald eagles soar. I wonder what it must feel like to be so free, powerful, and sure of the world around you. Gordon comes up to my room and sits on my bed. "Do you know," he says, "We are poor because of you? I am down to three of my five trucks because social services made me stay home, off the road, during the investigation."

Coming from Barbara, this would have stung. Coming from my dad, it's crushing.

"Poor because of you." These four short words are yet another reason to fear making a mistake. Yet another reason to fear speaking out. Yet another reason to ask, "What's wrong with me?"

GEMS OF WISDOM FOR CHAMPIONS

The words and actions of those I held in high regard shaped my self-worth. While their words have etched memories, it's the empowerment I derive from them that carves my path. Ask yourself: Are the mirrors in your life reflecting your truest, most empowered self?

I've stood on the precipice of expression, my heart's whisper held hostage by unsaid words. Fear? Maybe. Uncertainty? Probably. Yet, in understanding what chains my voice, I find the keys to unleash it. Where might freeing your voice take you today?

To me, the bald eagles soaring are emblems of unbridled freedom and might. They're not just birds; they're reminders of where I see myself. What symbols or metaphors represent freedom to you? And in what areas of your life do you seek that freedom? And are you ready to chase that horizon?

Free Bonus Training: "Crush It by Finding Your Voice:"
Access at PatriciaBartell.com/bonus

Six

THE UNDENIABLE POWER OF GETTING BACK UP

"In the eyes of those who truly love us,
we are never out of place."
—Patricia Bartell

*I*n all the months I'm ghosted by the Bartells, I miss my brothers' company the most. It had always been the three of us against the world. I adored them and would have done anything to be their third musketeer. In the early years, I often settle for being their third wheel instead.

We have a white dog called Cora. And for some reason, if you shout the word 'stick,' Cora runs in whatever direction you send her as if hunting a jackrabbit in a Formula One car with all the intensity of a high-speed chase. One day, Kenny and James get it into their heads to harness a toboggan to Cora, jump in it, shout 'stick,' and get free rides. "Tricia," they ask invitingly, "you wanna get in?" I never say no to my brothers. "Stick," they shout, and off Cora goes. Kenny and James love their genius idea until they realize Cora is going in the wrong direction. She is headed straight toward the wire fence with no sign of slowing down. With seconds to spare, I roll from the toboggan, averting a messy death by decapitation.

Another time, they're shooting coffee cans with long rifles. I ask if I can join in. "Sure, Tricia," they say, handing me the heavy rifle with a caliber and power load guaranteeing maximum recoil, which they fail to mention. As soon as I pull the trigger, the kickback almost takes my shoulder off. "It's gone, it's gone," I think to myself, referring to my burning arm. By miracle alone, my shoulder was neither 'gone' nor dislocated, and my brothers stared wide-eyed at each other, realizing the important detail they'd accidentally omitted.

My brothers were never intentionally mean to me. They had simply not heard my side of the Neilanne Cooper story. Little by little, trust is rebuilt, and little by little, they start speaking to me again. I am, once more, the sidekick to their exploits.

Like any Montana farm girl, I know how to semi-break horses. But I'm reluctant to break in my horse, Sassy, properly. Inspired by the Lone Ranger and wanting to impress my brothers, I make her rear up while yelling, "Hi ho, Silver!" Sassy is my Silver. I've trained her to kneel alongside the fence. I lead her to it, hoist myself up, then lower myself onto her bare back with no saddle. One day, I want to ride on our dirt roads. But Sassy has other ideas; she's not in the mood. She refuses, rears, loses her balance, and falls on my left leg. I'm sure it's broken. Daddy happens to be home; he runs to swoop me up and takes me into the house to examine my leg. "It's fine," he concludes. "Now," he says, "You go right back out there and get back on that horse."

At that moment, his tough love confused me. Later, I understood. Those words were branded onto me, "Get back on that horse." Before I experienced success after success, I first had to learn never to give up.

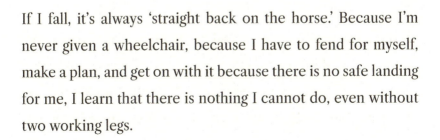

Gold Nugget

Before I experienced success after success,
I first had to learn never to give up.

If I fall, it's always 'straight back on the horse.' Because I'm never given a wheelchair, because I have to fend for myself, make a plan, and get on with it because there is no safe landing for me, I learn that there is nothing I cannot do, even without two working legs.

I even go downhill skiing with my brothers.

Big Mountain, with its beautiful veined, varied ski slopes, is only a two-hour drive from the farm. I use specialized crutches made from lightweight aluminum, designed to grip around the wrists. They have small skis attached to the end of the poles with metal claws on the bottom to dig into the snow and provide braking power. They came with wider-than-normal 'assisted skis' to give me better balance, and at the front tip, a thin bar connected the skis so I wouldn't be doing any splits on the slopes. My brothers initially help me on the Bunny Hills. I use my arms, apply pressure to the crutches, and shift my weight to navigate the terrain. I must learn fast because they are ready to take me to the real hills. Soon, I'm chasing them on the downslopes. It's exhilarating.

Kenny and James teach me to be tough. But they are kind, too.

We have only one bathroom in the entire sprawling house. It's on the ground floor at the base of the staircase, and on mornings and evenings, we line up like an ethnically diverse, disheveled version of the Von Trapp family, waiting our turn to use it.

In the early years, we all crowd in together. Kenny and James are strong and muscular and can out-bench-press the best of them. I am small for my age, and although I don't yet know it, I have typical Bolivian features: a moon-shaped face and almond-shaped eyes. Standing with them at the bathroom basins, I stare in the mirror and moan, "I don't look like anyone."

"Yes, you do," says Kenny with a gentleness I've never heard before. "You look like us. You have brown skin, black eyes, and dark hair. You look like us." It is the loveliest thing anyone has ever said to me.

GEMS OF WISDOM FOR CHAMPIONS

In the playfulness of innocent moments, I've discovered profound truths about myself. Those fleeting, light-hearted exchanges with loved ones have often painted the most vivid portraits of my capabilities. What mirror moments have revealed your potential?

Once, feeling like an outsider, I discovered an inner landscape that was rich and vast. The edges of discomfort, being that "third wheel," led me to a deeper self-awareness. It's in those raw, out-of-place moments that I truly met myself. Where have your edges taken you?

With my brothers by my side, I've dared to soar higher. They've been my challengers, my cheerleaders, pushing me to territories uncharted. Everyone has that force in their life, someone who nudges them into the vast expanse of possibilities. Who's been the wind beneath your wings?

Seven

FROM SHADOWS TO THE SPOTLIGHT

"Music is not just a set of notes; it's an emotion, an escape, and a friend in dark times."
—Patricia Bartell

*I*n the darkest of days, the accordion is my lifeline. I escape into my music.

I did not have my accordion at Shriners nor in foster care. Now home, I'm eventually allowed to resume lessons with Ruth. It doesn't take me long to catch up to James. I am coordinated, my fingers are agile, and I have upper body strength unusual for my age.

I can tell that James is frustrated. He says he prefers playing the slower, Western cowboy songs, but I know it's because my fingers are faster. For the first time, I've found something that I'm better at than he is, something that I am actually good at.

Ruth often says, "You know it's not gonna be long before you outplay me, and you will need a different teacher." But for now, she is all I've got. (What I inherit from Ruth, I realize many years later, is more valuable than technical finesse: She instills in me a knowing that music must be fun to learn. It's my Academy's governing principle today and how we teach our students.)

Ruth enlists James and me to play alongside her, usually accompanied by a bass and drummer, at open dances for people over sixty doing polkas and waltzes or for nursing homes and retirement homes. The sight of a small girl on crutches and her brother playing the accordion warms the hearts of the old folk, and we become circuit favorites.

Barbara is often complimented on our good behavior. We are indeed very well-behaved. We would never dare raise our voices, speak out of turn, act out, punch one another, run, skip, or sing with abandon. We stand still, we are silent, we say please and thank you, and we speak only when spoken to. We behave out of fear. Even so, Barbara is pleased with the praise; we're portraying the Bartells favorably with the Missoula community.

For this reason, Ruth can convince Barbara that I am good enough to compete, and Barbara agrees to enroll me in the Kimberley International Old Time Accordion Competition (KIOTAC) in Canada. And just like that, a door opens to a whole new world.

It's not so much the idea of competing that excites me; it is the knowledge that my hero, Myron Floren, will perform at the five-day festival. I count down to the competition the way other kids count down to Christmas.

Eventually, it arrived in the second week of July 1990. Barbara, Gordon, and eight children pile into a rented motorhome and set out on the four-hour journey from Charlo to the Kimberley, in the southeastern corner of British Columbia, north of the US Border.

The road trip is my looking glass, wardrobe, and platform 9 3/4, while KIOTAC is my Wonderland, Narnia, and Hogwarts rolled into one.

As we enter the town, we're met by the sounds of music from all directions. There are people dressed in Dirndls and Lederhosen, motorhomes lining the sides of the road as far as the eye can see, and impromptu performances everywhere you look. It's electric; tens of thousands of people converged on a remote little town, brought together by their shared love of the accordion.

The festival's heart is a converted hockey stadium with a bright green stage. In the arena, competitions occur all day, concerts all evening, and dances throughout the night.

When Myron performs, it's packed to capacity, and I have a seat in the front row. Finally, I get to see my hero in real life, not on TV, and not just for one song but for a whole hour. I don't want to miss one bellow shake, tremolo, or bass run. I'm afraid to even blink. Deep inside, I want to be on that stage playing with Myron. What a dream that would be!

The campground, where we park our motorhome, is also a bustling activity hub. I am left to roam free and follow the music as if entranced by a hundred Pied Pipers. People are drawn to me; the uncommon sight of a friendly little girl on crutches who plays a mean polka with fingers like lightning, the bellow shake of a man three times her size, and artistry beyond her years. Wherever I stop, I'm handed an accordion and invited to join. Two players inevitably become four, then ten. Spouses and children gather round, and before you know it, there's a huge crowd bonding by the bonfire, singing under the stars, and enveloped by the nostalgic sounds of accordions. I've found my happy place.

The old timers share their tricks and techniques with me and offer encouragement I've never known. I love the camaraderie and community. I feel accepted for the first time.

A DREAM COME TRUE

I return to KIOTAC many times over the next decade. In the early years, I go with the Bartells, and later, I'll hitch a lift, sleep in spare beds in friends' hotel rooms, whatever it takes. But it's what happens on the final day of that first year that determines so much of my future music trajectory.

I'm walking back to the campsite when I realize I'm being followed by a pickup truck. It idles beside me. A kind-looking man leans out the window and introduces himself as Gordon Schmitt.

"Where are you camped?" he asks.

"Just there," I point. "You can follow me."

We chat on the way, and when we get to the campsite, he hands me a sheet of music. "I want you to learn this," he says. I turn it over. It's the *Champagne Polka*, arranged and handwritten by Myron Floren. I don't know what to say. I stare from the paper to the truck and back to the paper as Gordon drives away.

Gordon and I become pen pals. Over the next year, I write him long letters about my progress with the accordion, and he writes back.

The following July, my family returns to Canada for the second time and stations at the same site as the previous year. I must help set up camp, but all I want to do is go find Gordon. I step out of the motorhome, and unbelievably, he is talking to my dad.

"I have a surprise for Patricia," he says.

"Patricia," he asks, "can you be at the arena at 6 pm this evening?"

I look at my dad with raised eyebrows and an inflection. "Yes," I answer. My dad smiles.

"Good," says Gordon Schmitt with a twinkle in his eye. "Tonight, you are going to play with Myron Floren." I can hardly believe what I'm hearing. Play with Myron Floren, me? I look at my dad, I look at Gordon, I could pinch myself. Really? I'm going to play with Myron Floren.

Gold Nugget

When someone sees potential in you, they're not just looking at what you are but at what you could become.

I'm at the arena well before 6 pm, wearing my best concert dress, which I have sewn myself. Seven of us from across the American Pacific Northwest have been handpicked to play with Myron. We're taken through the evening's proceedings. When Myron starts playing *Stars and Stripes Forever*, that's our cue. We're to get up from our seats and go to the back of the stage. Then Myron will introduce us as "The Seven of the Best from the Northwest," and we will file onto the stage. Six steps lead onto the stage; I'll go first because I'm on crutches. Someone will carry my accordion. I will sit beside Myron with the rest of The Best behind us. We will play *The Champagne Polka*, *The Beer Barrel Polka*, *God Bless America*, and *O Canada*.

Myron comes to the rehearsal and shakes my hand. My idol tells me he is happy to have me in the band. I'm starstruck, lost for words. I stare at his accordion. It's beautiful and much heavier than I imagined, the one he uses on The Lawrence Welk Show.

We finish rehearsing, and the audience filters in. I'm again sitting in the front row, but this time, I can hardly concentrate for the excitement. Before my eyes is my hero. And I'm going to perform with him; we're going to play a song he wrote, one that he's only ever played on TV, and I've been practicing all year.

We line up in front of the six steps. My body is shaking. I see some people sitting on the side bleachers pointing at me. I'm sure my shaking is obvious. I am so excited. The men behind me are full of smiles. They know that my dream is to play with Myron Floren. And it's about to come true.

We start the *Champagne Polka*. It's a technical piece. I'm lost in concentration. When I look up, I meet Myron's eyes, and he grins. It's as if we are collaborators or members of a secret club, a world nobody else can access or understand.

Next is the *Beer Barrel Polka*, a score notorious for its challenging bellow shakes. The bellow shake is an accordion technique that creates a rapid rhythmic tremolo effect. The mechanics involve opening and closing the bellows quickly while simultaneously holding down one or more keys on the keyboard. The faster and more complex the bellow shakes, the greater the arm strength, coordination, timing, and effort required to execute it cleanly. Whenever Myron performs the *Beer Barrel's* bellow shake, the audience, appreciating its difficulty, erupts in applause. But this time, all attention is on me.

He watches intently, and when I'm done, he leans back and gives me that Myron Floren wide-as-the-Flathead-River smile.

I feel as if I'm going to explode with happiness. This is a new feeling for me.

GEMS OF WISDOM
FOR CHAMPIONS

Music wasn't just melody to me; it was the one place I could lose myself and live without judgment. We all have that refuge, a passion or hobby, that shelters us in storms. In my darkest moments as a child, it was a note, a chord, a song, that became my lifeline. What is that for you?

Someone saw a fire in me before it was even a spark. Their belief kindled my potential. It's a gift we all have the power to give. Who around you is just waiting for your faith to ignite their future?

My life's tapestry is woven with the wisdom of mentors. Every thread represents guidance, support, and insight from those who've shaped me. It's a reminder that we don't walk our path alone. Who's been the weaver of your journey's fabric?

Eight

WHERE LIFE'S PATHS MEET LOSS AND LEADS TO LOVE

*"Every moment in life has its purpose—some teach us
to love, some to surrender, and some to leverage.*
—Patricia Bartell

In *The Last Best Place*, Montana-born author William Kittredge writes, "Deep in the far heart of my upbringing, a crew of us sixteen-year-old lads was driven crazy with ill-defined midsummer sadness, by the damp, sour-smelling sweetness of night-time alfalfa fields, an infinity of stars and moonglow, and no girlfriends whatsoever. Frogs croaked in the lonesome swamp ... Travel the highways in Montana, and you will see little white crosses along the dangerous curves, marking places where travelers have died ... most of them searching and unable to name what it was they were missing at home."

Kenny is on his motorcycle, heading back home early one evening. James is following in a pick-up truck. There is a hill, and at the bottom of the hill, an intersection. A driver approaching perpendicular to the downhill doesn't notice Kenny turning and T-bones him. James later tells us that he saw what was about to happen, saw it in slow motion, but could do nothing to prevent it. Kenny dies in his arms.

James and Kenny did everything together, they were inseparable. James sinks into a deep depression. He just doesn't care about anything anymore; life holds no excitement. He shuts down, acts out, and starts getting into trouble. I feel devastatingly alone.

In some ways, I lose both my brothers at that intersection.

Gold Nuggets

Our strongest stories aren't just about survival but about rising from the ashes.

It is the last dance of the last day of the Kimberley International Old Time Accordion Competition when news reaches us of Kenny's death. All the awards are done, the concerts are finished, and we're hanging out on the dancefloor. I hear my dad's name over the PA system. "Gordon Bartell, there is a phone call for you." I watch my dad go out then come back. I watch him talk to Barbara. I watch her go out. Then my dad returns, gathers the children, and says, "Come on guys, we're gonna leave. We gotta go." I'm the last one back to the van. Barbara is upfront with her head in her hands. The children are in the back, crying. "Kenny's dead," they tell me between tears.

Living on a farm, you witness the whole cycle of life. But Kenny's is my first experience of human death.

There is an open viewing of the casket in a little chapel alongside the funeral home. We line up and go in individually to see Kenny for the last time.

I stare at his body. I take in his navy suit jacket. I notice that his hair has been combed flat. It's not the way he would wear it. This is not him. He is not here. This is just a shell of bones and skin. I feel nothing. I'm blank. I have no questions and no emotions.

All my life, I've been told what to do, what to think, and how I should feel. My values have been branded into me by Barbara. I've never been given a choice, opinion, or preference. Life has been done to me. I am ordered; I obey. I'm knocked down; I get up. I do my duty. Standing before Kenny's corpse, I have no language for grief or vocabulary for love or loss. After all, how do you teach a blind girl 'blue'?

RELIGION VERSUS FAITH

Ours is a Christian home. I can tell you every Bible story, allegory, psalm, and scripture; evangelical programs run on our TV like the backdrop music underscoring an epic drama. I've grown up in the Assemblies of God, a Christian denomination founded on the core beliefs that we are all sinners, born into a fallen world, and that Salvation is received through repentance and faith in the Lord Jesus Christ. From my perspective, there is Gordon: loving but remote, silent when home, but mostly absent. And Barbara: judgmental, omniscient, and strict. I unconsciously adopt an idea of God as remote, unforgiving, concerned with rules and punishment, a deity of stern demeanor and disapproval, waiting for me to make a mistake and punish me accordingly. In profound theological reversal, my notion of God is created in my parents' image.

No matter how hard I try, I never measure up. I must be doing something wrong. I must not be good enough for Him to love me. He is always watching me; any misstep or mistake could provoke ire and punishment. I have to strive to be better.

Worship, usually on Sundays and mostly at home, is conducted in the living room, where we gather to listen to a televised sermon and pray collectively. At the end of the makeshift service, either Gordon or Barbara offers an invitation to "ask Jesus to come into your heart and life, to be the Lord and Savior of your life." It is possibly the only time we're ever given a choice.

I am only seven when I put my hand up. I do want Jesus in my life. I understand that I need a savior. I want to be good. I want to give myself to God. They lead me in prayer. I know the words and repeat them. But afterward, I don't feel any different.

Sometimes, when Barbara isn't in a doctrinal deadlock with the officiating pastor, we go to one of the local churches. Filing out of a newer church in Charlo, the pastor puts his hand on my shoulder and kindly says three words I've never heard, "I love you." I'm taken aback and immediately think, "No, you don't. You don't even know me." As a survivor of childhood trauma, I am hypersensitized to authenticity and the vagaries of truth and falsity.

I know the pastor means well, but I have a huge problem with the notion of 'love.' It's not a word I hear from my parents, ever. The closest semantic proximity to 'love' is the phrase, 'We care.' "We do this because we care. We feed you because we care. We clothe you because we care. We teach you the value of hard work because we care." Barbara punishes me because she cares.

I am nine years old when I get the first intimation of a loving God who might want our joy, and not merely to bestow judgment. My older siblings, Callie and Phyllis, pray in the living room. I'm sitting on the couch, watching. "Would you like us to pray for you, to receive the Holy Spirit?" they ask. They are always kind to me.

"Yes," I answer.

At first, I passively watch my sisters pray. They are speaking a secret code of seemingly nonsensical syllables and streams of consciousness; they are 'speaking in tongues.'

Almost all Pentecostal denominations believe that the 'initial evidence' of Spirit baptism manifests as speaking in an unknown language. I'm familiar with the phenomenon, but I've never experienced it.

Now, unexpectedly, I feel a strange sensation in my throat. A dam breaks inside me, and a river of words pours forth, words to a language I've never spoken. I'm euphoric, radiant, awash with wonder, plugged into an electrical charge. This is peace. This is acceptance. This is joy. Given that I have never known love, it's unfathomable what recesses of the soul, what ancient memories these feelings spring from, but if I know nothing else, I know this now: God is real, and God is Love.

Gold Nugget

True faith transcends rituals and rules;
it's a deep, personal bond with the Divine.

For many years, this remains an isolated incident. It sets the foundation for my spiritual journey based on a direct relationship between God and me that will flourish once I leave the farm. But for now, God is still the abstract, unforgiving

North Star of Barbara's religious searching. And all I want is to belong.

At fourteen, I'm sent to Bible camp. It's fun to be with other kids and do fun camp things. I am surrounded by other teens who seem to enjoy life and God. We pray together, play together, and sing worship songs together. I find myself laughing a lot, and I catch myself thinking, "Is this allowed? To have this much fun with God?"

My favorite TV evangelist is not the one who gives the best sermons; it's the one who shows inserts of his family in Florida. He has a boy and a girl, who appear to bask in their parents' nurturing care. "Wouldn't it be fun to be part of that family?" I think. I dream of running away to Florida to live with them.

The idea of running away comes to me via Kevin. Kevin was the oldest adopted brother whom I never knew. He was gone when I arrived, and his name was only ever mentioned in oblique references by my parents. They speak of how 'difficult' he was, but I'm impressed by the courage and ingenuity of his great escapes. Kevin is mythic. I don't know what became of him, but his disappearance has planted a seed: If he could escape, perhaps I could too.

I have never liked the expression: 'To run as fast your legs can carry you.' I am not going anywhere fast.

GEMS OF WISDOM FOR CHAMPIONS

Every challenge I've met carved a new strength within me. It's not about the trials we face but the lessons we extract. For every storm I've weathered, I've found an anchor within, reminding me of my resilience and power.

My faith is not borrowed; it's chosen. While many beliefs were whispered to me, it's the ones I've tested and embraced that resonate deeply. Faith isn't about acceptance; it's about asking questions, discovery, and alignment with the deepest truths of my soul.

Dreams aren't distant; they're only decisions away. Longing for love and acceptance isn't about finding the perfect place but crafting it. With every choice, I shape my world. The life I desire? It starts with the next step I take. Don't sit and wait for life to happen, take imperfect action. As Tony Robbins would say, "Progress equals happiness."

Nine

THE INVISIBLE CHAINS OF DEPRESSION

*"Amidst the echoes of our past, it's a decision
we make to find the strength to write our future."
—Patricia Bartell*

Competing at Kimberley International Old Time Accordion Competition shows me another way of being and belonging. I understand what it is to be seen, heard, and admired.

It's like falling in love.

Returning from Canada each year, I am on a high. Lit up.

95

There is something inside me that is excited. Everything is beautiful.

Then I have to go home. And I go quiet.

Barbara can see this. And I guess deep down, she wants me to be that girl who smiles all the time in Canada, at home, too. Maybe she even realizes there is something she just cannot give me. She threatens, "If you're going to be like this when we get back, we just won't go anymore."

In Canada, I am given attention. I am everybody's favorite. But I know I've won that attention because I've played well and earned it. It's still conditional. And it can't compensate for what I'm missing at home.

Like a movie star, adored by her fans and miserable behind closed doors. Like a successful CEO admired by her colleagues but forgotten by her family. I crave close, authentic connection.

If I perform well, people are happy, including the Bartells. If I work hard and exceed expectations, there is peace in the Bartell household. And so, I withdraw further and further into both work and music: chores, practice, and performance.

By the age of fifteen, the death of Kenny, my inability to reconcile the light of Kimberley with the shadows of Charlo, the trauma of foster care, my experience with Child Protection Services, months of marginalization, unpredictable beatings, imminent punishment, and always, the ever-present, nagging question, "What is wrong with me?" all stack up. And I fall from a mountain into despair. I have no language of self-care and no tools for coping. I cannot find answers; I don't even know the questions. There is no way out. All I have is constant, pressing, suffocating heartache and circular thoughts of ending it all.

Gold Nugget

In our darkest moments,
we discover the essence of resilience.

I'm sometimes dropped at Costco to do the monthly shopping on my own while the others run errands around town. My grocery list consists of staples and various non-consumables. Still, we're a household of twelve - thirteen when dad's home— and three carts must be filled.

It's an hour to Missoula and another hour back to Charlo, and there's lots of work waiting for us on the farm. So, the challenge is always to get everything done in the shortest amount of time. For me, it's a challenge multiplied and intensified by the number of carts I have to push. Three carts mean three times as much supermarket mileage. I push one cart from the canned food aisle to the bottom of the bread and pasta aisle, then return to fetch the second and third carts. I take one cart up and down the aisle while the others stand like helpless and expectant children impatiently waiting for check out. I sometimes ask for assistance to reach the higher shelves, but I can carry heavy items like five-liter cartons or bulk boxes of detergents. My fingers are strong from playing the accordion; my arms are strong from farm work. I find a way. I always find a way. This is perhaps the greatest, albeit inadvertent, gift Barbara gives me: 'Can't' is not an option.

Costco always has demonstration tables in various aisles. And on this day, a lady is promoting leather pouches and other accessories for men. Despite the race against time, I stop to look at the display. She greets me and says something like 'protecting my family' and that 'my husband can use it when he goes hunting.' I asked her how old she thinks I am. "Ma'am," she says, "I'd say the late forties. No, no, maybe early fifties." Years of fear, stress, and sorrow have taken their toll. Depression makes me look old. It hangs on me like a washed-out flannel shirt and dirty baggy jeans. And I don't care; I don't care much about anything. "Oh," I say, walking away, "I'm sixteen."

Gold Nugget

Adversity doesn't build character; it reveals it.

At the depth of my depression, home alone one day, I come downstairs and mindlessly pick up the remote and flip on the TV. Talking in tongues is only one of the gifts of the Charismatic or Pentecostal traditions. Another is the Word of Knowledge, the information given to someone directly from God.

On television, an evangelist gets a word of knowledge, "There's a girl that is watching me, and you're very depressed; you're suicidal, and you're wanting to end it all," he says as if looking straight at me, through me, and into my soul. "And God is telling me right now that he's setting you free from today." And with that, I feel something instantly lift from me as if I've been freed from a terrible burden. I know my pain has a purpose and that I must stick around long enough to understand it. I am still sad, but I never contemplate suicide again.

In her defense, Barbara seems to be genuinely disturbed by my unhappiness. But for her, 'depression' is unchristian, right down there with 'resentful' and 'ungrateful.' In her religious cosmology, it is an indictment of my sinful nature. And the solution is repentance.

So, one day, we pile into the red family van and drive three and a half hours to Elijah House in Idaho.

Elijah House is an inner healing ministry that works through prophetic prayer and pastoral counseling to 'bind broken hearts.' Its credo is: 'Bad fruits come from bitter roots.'

I have accepted that I need deliverance. There is something wrong with me; I'm the reason the family is poor and the cause of many of its problems. I have issues. And I believe that the team at Elijah House is sincerely trying to figure out, in the most well-meaning way, 'how they can help this girl' – meaning me. But at some point, the counselor asks me a question related to

Barbara, and I think, "Oh no, this could turn bad real fast!"

I fear getting into trouble or doing something wrong, as the punishment will be brutal.

The counselors probably know a whole lot more than they're letting on. The role of the mother and how parents should love their children is a big part of Elijah House's spiritual psychology, and I suspect they may have tried to raise this with Barbara.

Although I dutifully read all the literature and repeat all the prescribed prayers, Barbara claims that they have failed to fix me and that we are "never going there again." We never do dig down to the "bitter root" of my sad fruit.

GEMS OF WISDOM FOR CHAMPIONS

Each challenge I've faced has been a hidden gift. It's easy to see the pain, but within that pain lies immense strength, insight, and understanding. Those scars? They're not marks of defeat; they're badges of resilience and growth. When life pushes you down, don't just rise; soar with the newfound wisdom it offers.

On the surface, every challenge seems just like a roadblock. But I've learned to delve deeper, to seek the story beneath the story. When you scratch beyond the surface, you find the root, and that's where true healing and understanding begins. Challenges aren't just tests; they're lessons waiting to be deciphered.

Adversity? I've chosen to see it differently. Instead of walls, I see stepping stones. Instead of setbacks, I see learnings. Every challenge is an invitation—not to retreat but to redefine.

Ten

EMBRACING THE NAME, CLAIMING THE STAGE

"Music bridges the gap between generations,
creating timeless bonds."
—Patricia Bartell

*D*espite the fallout of returning from Canada to the realities of farm life, Kimberley does give me something to look forward to each year. And I am more driven than ever. Before, playing was an escape; now, I have reason to push myself. I want to live up to not only Myron's but all of my new friends' standards.

There is Gordon Schmitt and Mike Belitz, a strong-shouldered serious businessman with a twinkle in his eye who gives me the accordion I will play until college; Odie Odenbrett, a gentle giant, a kind teddy bear of a man; and Jim Howerton, who becomes my teacher when Ruth retires.

Ruth is getting frail. I've technically surpassed her, and she's happy to pass the reins to Jim. So, every other month I set off ninety minutes westward on Route 212, past Flathead Lake, turning north on Route 93 to Kalispell, where Jim lives. Jim works as a conductor on the railways by day. By night, he composes. When not on the trains, he produces music and sells his cassettes. Jim is a beautiful accordion player with a sharp ear and a quick eye, but he is not a trained teacher. He is simply prepared to show me all he knows.

My sister Sarah lives in Kalispell, too. Sometimes Barbara drives me and visits Sarah while I have a lesson with Jim. Other times, James takes me. James has lost interest in the accordion; he only ever played because Barbara insisted that he choose an instrument. He did compete in our second year at KIOTAC, where comparing himself to the other more competitive players, he came up short of his expectations. And since Kenny's death, the music has stopped altogether for James. He takes me because he enjoys driving. I feel that if he could, he would drive straight into the horizon and disappear. As I get older, I drive myself.

I never liked my name, 'Patricia,' until James and I competed in the duet category at KIOTAC. We were waiting backstage to be announced. I hear, "Please welcome Phillip and Patricia Bartell." "Wow!" I think, "That's a strong name for a performer: Patricia Bartell." From that moment onwards, I embrace it. Not 'Pat' mind you, nor 'Patty' but Patricia. Patricia Bartell is a name destined for the stage!

I learn a lot from Jim, but the real masterclasses occur at Swan Lake, where several of my 'accordion-playing' elders and their spouses meet yearly for three days en route to KIOTAC. If you were to ask me the way to heaven, I'd tell you it's along Swan Highway, running through Swan Valley. And if you keep going all the way to the water, passing moose, elk, and mountain lions; fir, spruce, and pine forested hills; osprey and loons at the lake, you'll finally arrive at the cabins where my friends and I gather.

Gold Nugget
True mastery is not just in playing, but in listening – to the notes, the silences, and the wisdom shared.

Odie lets me take him on a jet ski. At 40 miles an hour, my long black hair forms a wake in the wind. I ride with all the confidence of a girl who has grown up breaking wild horses, manipulating heavy machinery, feeding farm animals, and keeping up with her Native American brothers. We make fires, eat, and talk about the competition. But it's the accordion we're all here for; the accordion crosses ages, absorbs all our sorrows, and expresses all our joy. The sweet, nostalgic, sometimes giddy, sometimes mournful song of the accordion is what bonds us.

My friends are mostly in their seventies and eighties, and they treat me as a grandparent does a grandchild. On my last visit to Swan Lake, my senior year, I play a piece for them that I've been practicing: "Dark Eyes." It will become one of my signature pieces and one of the scores I'll eventually play at the World Championships more than a decade later. They listen attentively. Someone whistles softly. Someone else says, "This girl has something." Then they all pipe in: "Watch the tempo." "Here, try this." "Do that..." Now we are jamming together. They want me to succeed.

GEMS OF WISDOM FOR CHAMPIONS

Every scar, every tear, every laughter line on our faces carries a story, a lesson, a whisper of the past. I've realized that each of us holds a treasure trove of insights that can illuminate someone else's path. There's someone younger, eager to learn, waiting for a role model like you. Don't just walk your journey; light up someone else's. The beauty of life isn't just in living our own stories but in shaping narratives for others with the wisdom we've gained.

There was this electrifying moment when someone reflected back to me a version of myself I had yet to see. It wasn't draped in flattery but in profound, genuine validation. Their words weren't just heard; they resonated, breaking old molds and casting me in a new light. Moments like these are more than mere compliments; they're awakenings. Treasure those epiphanies when someone else's belief in you fuels your belief in yourself. Because sometimes, it's through others' eyes that we truly see ourselves.

Eleven

REVEALING THE MUSIC TEACHER WITHIN

"Every teacher can transform a life;
every obstacle can teach a lesson."
—Patricia Bartell

At 16, I am sent to high school. At first, Barbara and Gordon enroll me in a private Christian Academy. The classes are small, and a boy called Dustin Long with piercing blue eyes becomes a friend to me. We take Spanish class together and laugh a lot. The social butterfly in me starts to open its wings. But it's fleeting: no public transport to and from the Academy poses a logistical problem for the Bartells. So, mid-year, I'm removed from the Academy and enrolled at the local high school in Charlo instead.

I don't want to go to Charlo High School. Public school means waking up even earlier to milk the cows and do my chores, leaving no time for accordion practice. My world feels like it's ending. But I have no choice. As is often the case, the decision has been made for me.

I stand in the freezing cold at the end of our snow-laden driveway, mindlessly snapping off icicle-coated strands of wet hair, waiting for the big yellow school bus, anticipating inevitable stares from the kids, some well-meaning, some not, who will later ask me, some kindly, some not, "What's wrong with you?"

When I arrive to the school, I'm given a little piece of paper telling me where my classes are. I don't want to be doing this at all. Finally, it's the last lesson of the day: band practice. I'm looking around, wondering where to go, when there appears in front of me a boy, blond with hair to his shoulders, handsome, friendly, a senior.

"Hey, aren't you Patricia Bartell?" he asks.

"Yeah," I answer.

"I know your brothers," he says.

"Oh, cool," I say.

"You look lost. Where are you headed?" he asks.

"Uhm, the band room," I answer.

"That's where I'm going. Come with me; I'll show you," he offers.

His name is Grant, and he plays the trumpet. Watching him warm up, hitting the high notes, I think, "That's an amazing instrument."

"I'd love to learn to play the trumpet like that," I say out loud.

"Well," he says, "I'm sure we can find one for you."

"Really?" I ask, knowing full well that there's no way my parents will invest in another musical instrument.

And that's when I meet Alicia Lipscomb, K-12 music teacher and the first woman to help put me on a path that leads away from the farm into a future of possibility.

Alicia gives me a school trumpet to use. I bury the mouthpiece in my pocket and don't tell anyone at home about it. I know that my parents cannot afford another instrument.

So, I practice when I'm alone, milking the cows.

Now and then, one of my brother's comments, "Did anyone

hear those strange noises coming from the cow shed? Sounded like a sick goose?" I say nothing.

But Alicia plays the role of the fairy godmother in more important ways. A term into my internment at Charlo High School, we have our first major concert. Alicia starts by setting the scene: "You're going to hear Patricia Bartell play today. She's only been with us a few months." She refers to me, several times, as an angel. She praises me for all the work I've done: "When I needed a piano accompaniment, Patricia stepped in. When I needed a trumpet player, Patricia stepped in. She plays the piano and the flute, too. And she plays the accordion like an angel." My dad is the only Bartell in the audience. And although I know he doesn't much like music, I couldn't be prouder.

Alicia plugs me straight into the school system and saves me. She encourages my talent in other ways, too. One day, an external examiner comes to the school to test our musicality and measure our potential to study music at the college level. The test is designed to reveal our understanding of basic music theory, concepts such as notation, rhythm, scales, and chords, and our aural skill: our ability to identify intervals, tempo, and melodies by ear. And, of course, the way we play.

Alicia comes to give me the results, "You scored really high," she says with a smile, "Even higher even than me in some areas."

But the real measure of Alicia's kindness is how she rescues me on 'Switch Day.'

Switch Day is the students' most anticipated day of the school year. On Switch Day, parents and students switch roles. A parent attends all their child's classes, and the child gets to stay home for the day. The kids have been talking about it for weeks. Knowing my family, I think, "This will never work."

At band practice, Alicia asks, "Who's coming in for you?

"No one," I say.

She gets it.

A few days later, she approaches me and says, "I have an idea. You're thinking about becoming a music teacher, right? Well, what if you and I switch? I'll do all your classes, and you can teach all my classes, from Kindergarten to Grade 12. Make lesson plans, bring your accordion, and show the kids how it works. You can even lead Junior High band practice; then I'll return and take Senior band practice with you. Okay?"

I have so much fun. I especially love working with the younger kids. I'm used to changing diapers, preparing feeding bottles, and taking charge of my younger siblings. So, when it came to classroom management, I know how to be the boss, organize, and get things done. The class aid, Kelly, is amazed. He tells me later, "Those kids behaved even better with you than they do with Alicia." I'm pretty sure it's because the kids are so fascinated with the accordion, but I thank him for his encouraging words.

By the end of the day, I have set my intention: to attend college and become a music teacher.

HEARTBREAK

Alicia Lipscomb gives me self-belief and, even better, hope, a dream, and a plan. But not even she can save me from a far more urgent and perplexing problem: boys.

No matter how angelically I play the accordion, flute, trumpet, or piano, no matter how tuned I am to "the fourth, the fifth, the minor fall, the major lift, the secret chord to please the Lord," there is no siren song to divert attention from my obvious disability. I might be Alicia Lipscomb's angel, but I have leg braces and crutches for wings.

I am taking part in a school play. One of the songs is "Have I told you lately that I love you." Perhaps it's the romance of the lyrics, or maybe the fact that he is tall, dark, and wears a forest ranger's uniform. Anyway, with unfathomable boldness, I point to this dad wearing a badge and gun holster who has been so kind to me throughout the rehearsal, and I say, 'That's the kind of man I want to marry one day!'

I do not know whether someone tells him or if he hears me say it, but the ranger-dad sweetly comes up to tell me that he has

114

a son and maybe he and I can go out together sometime. "You going to ask him?" I'm nervous, embarrassed, and excited all at the same time.

Later, coming round the corridor corner, I see them talking. I know it's about me. And the look of horror on the boy's face stops me in my tracks. It's as if he's been asked to eat poison. I know that I've seen something I shouldn't have. I go back the way I came. And in my chest, I feel an old, familiar heartache. Again, that feeling of being unwanted. Again, that question: "What is wrong with me?"

Then comes Junior Year Homecoming. The boys are inviting all the girls. Except me. I tell myself it's because I'm still new to the school. Maybe my science teacher's telling herself the same thing because she asks me after class, "Are you going to the dance?" I tell her I don't have a partner. "If you could go with someone, who would it be?" she probes. I don't know how to answer, so I point to Tyler. Tyler lives on the farm that neighbors ours. From what I've seen, he is a hard-working, good kid. But mostly, he is in my line of vision when I'm asked the question and is the first name that comes to mind. The teacher says she's going to talk to Tyler.

She does, and later that evening, she calls me at home.

But it's Barbara who picks up the phone.

"Why are you calling my home? Why do you want to speak to

Patricia? If something's the matter, I'm the one to talk to, right? Not her, right?" She finally forces the reason for the phone call from the teacher.

The teacher tries explaining that she was just hoping to put me together with a partner for the dance, and that she just wanted to help. Barbara thinks I've put the teacher up to this, and she is livid.

Barbara is upset, the teacher is upset, and I'm in big trouble.

Although I'm already 17, Barbara believes I'm too young for devilish things like dancing and dates, and I'm not allowed to go. Which doesn't matter anymore because Tyler said 'no.'

Gold Nugget

The dance of life isn't always to the rhythm we choose, but it's how we move that defines us.

I can attend my Senior Homecoming the following year, but Barbara picks the dress and the date. He is a seven-foot tall, skinny boy from Bulgaria who's only at Charlo High School for a semester. I had always thought that it would be fun and exciting when I eventually got to go to a dance. But this is dull and awkward and not at all what I'd dreamed of.

GEMS OF WISDOM FOR CHAMPIONS

We all have that one mentor or teacher who shifted the trajectory of our lives. Let me let you in on one of the most game-changing insights they gifted me: Our lives aren't molded by the knowledge we accumulate but by the wisdom we allow to resonate and take root. Every person you meet, every lesson you learn—embrace it. It might just be the pivot you've been searching for.

Disappointments and rejections? They're like echoes from the past, hitting on our deepest insecurities. But here's a revelation I've had: They aren't anchors but catalysts. They possess the power to either hold us down or propel us forward. And when those shadows of doubt creep in, I lean into strategies that help me rise above as a Champion. The secret? Embracing vulnerability and reframing it as an opportunity. It's not about escaping the pain but leaning into it, understanding its source, and transmuting it into strength. The next time life knocks you down, I challenge you to ask: "What's the lesson in this pain?" It's there, waiting to catapult you into a newer, stronger version of yourself.

Vulnerability. It's that raw, unguarded moment where we stand exposed, our true selves laid bare. Yet, in those moments of softness, I've found an unmatched strength. For it's not in shielding our hearts that we find power, but in opening them up. So, in your moments of doubt and uncertainty, look inward and to those around you. Find your anchor, be it within or in the compassionate arms of a loved one. Always remember: Strength isn't about not breaking; it's about bending and bouncing back even more resilient.

Twelve

WHEN REJECTION AND HEARTBREAK HITS HOME

"Music can change the world because it can change people."
—Patricia Bartell

The accordion is a force of nature. In its playing, it expresses something fundamental about the universe; it sings the bittersweet beauty of life. It is my shield against loneliness and longing. It is my passport to freedom, to a world beyond the farm.

In some ways, I am like an accordion: portable but cumbersome, always slightly out of place, slightly foreign, and always a bit misunderstood. Even so, I like to think it is my accordion, not me, that is rejected from every university to which I apply. And I apply to many. For every letter of application, there is a letter of refusal: 'Dear Patricia, Thank you but... on further consideration.... we regret to inform you...' They all have an explanation: "We don't have a program for the accordion, we don't have professors to teach the accordion, we don't have an adjudicating body for the accordion." That is what they say. This is what they mean: "The accordion is an instrument of the working class, lowbrow, lacking the refinement and pedigree of, say, piano or violin. It belongs to the backrooms of dance halls and cafes, not in the hallowed halls of our academic institutions."

In the cultural divide between educated and uneducated, the accordion is relegated to second-class status. But I will not leave my accordion behind. I cannot; it's too much a part of me. A friend urges me to apply to Whitworth University in Spokane again. They tell me to contact the Chair of the Music Department to plead my case. I do. It works.

The Board of Directors convened, debated, and decided to give me a chance. I audition for both piano and accordion. There are caveats: 1. I have to find a teacher capable of instructing accordion at the university level, who the university must approve. 2. At the end of my sophomore year, I will have to perform for the entire Department of Music, who will vote on whether I can graduate with a Bachelor of Arts degree in

Accordion Performance. If not, I'll have to default to Piano. 3. Whitworth is a private university. I will have to take out student loans to pay for my tuition. It's a gamble I'm willing to take.

Gold Nugget

The melody of our passion often leads to the rhythm of our destiny.

Alicia Lipscomb has prepared me sufficiently in piano to pass my entry audition. I even play enough ragtime and Chopin to win a $1000 piano scholarship. As for the accordion, I know just the man to teach me: a stern Estonian with a tragic past that clouds his face like a physical wound. Displaced in World War Two, he arrived in America alone as a teenage immigrant with only three dollars in his pocket and his father's old accordion in his case.

At KIOTAC, his students are technically strong and the ones to beat. If anybody can get me to college accordion level, he can.

It's 1996, and we head out to Spokane in the red van. This time to drop me off at Whitworth University. I have with me a black plastic garbage bag that contains all my worldly belongings. I'm taken to my new dorm room. As soon as we know I'm in the right room, my family immediately leaves. I watch the red van drive off into the distance. A chapter closes, and a new one opens.

STRONGEST IN THE PLACES WE'VE BEEN BROKEN

In my second year of university, the question of formals comes up again. Having grown up with brothers, I am comfortable and natural around boys, and they often come to me for advice. Whitworth is a conservative Presbyterian university. My friends share my values; we hang out in cafes and go to church together, and it's all good, clean fun.

I have one friend with whom I hang out often. We have long, meaningful discussions together. He is a phenomenal artist who sketches sensitive portraits, religious iconography, and drawings of Jesus's hand with nails. He is creative, thoughtful, and a good conversationalist. We are close friends, and it feels easy to suggest that we go to the dance together, even though he has told me I'm not his type many times. He prefers tall girls with blond hair, porcelain skin, and long athletic limbs, not exactly Barbie, but close. I am not that.

Still, he happily agrees to go to the formal with me. Afterward, the two of us go back to his apartment. He is explaining the meaning behind all his art hanging on the walls. Inspired by his artistry, feeling good about having had a 'date' for the dance, and encouraged by his best friend who has suggested we'd make a great couple, I summon the courage to ask if he'd like to take our friendship further.

He is sweet, and he tells me that, in many ways, I'm the perfect gal, everything he would want in a wife. But I wouldn't be able to go biking, hiking, or any of those outdoor things. And he really wants to be able to do those kinds of activities with his wife one day.

And there it is. The pain in my chest, the broken-hearted girl on the ninth step, the crushing feeling that I'm not good enough to be wanted or loved, the question, "What is wrong with me?"

Coincidentally, his best friend asked me to talk at a youth group gathering the following evening. I phone him to tell what has happened and that I'm not up to it. "Trish," he says, "it would be the best thing for you. You need to share what you have come through. You've overcome so much, and this is just one more thing."

I'm heartbroken. But I summon up the courage to go. I stand before the youth group and tell them, "Walking with crutches is hard. It has caused people to underestimate, ignore, and reject me. But where would I be without them?

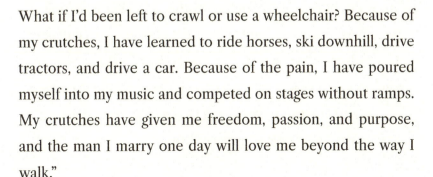

Gold Nugget

Strength emerges not from perfection, but resilience.

What if I'd been left to crawl or use a wheelchair? Because of my crutches, I have learned to ride horses, ski downhill, drive tractors, and drive a car. Because of the pain, I have poured myself into my music and competed on stages without ramps. My crutches have given me freedom, passion, and purpose, and the man I marry one day will love me beyond the way I walk."

GEMS OF WISDOM FOR CHAMPIONS

We've all walked through the storm of societal prejudices and judgments. It's a journey of navigating other people's perceptions and expectations. But understand this: It's not about them, it's about us. It's about owning our stories, reclaiming our power, and responding from a place of authenticity rather than just adapting. When you crush those preconceived notions with your genuine self, you not only empower your journey, but you pave the way for others to do the same. I challenge you as a Champion: Rise above and show the world your unparalleled uniqueness.

Rejection and setbacks? Oh, I've danced with them more times than I can count. But here's what I know: It's not the setback that defines you; it's the comeback. Every 'no' can fuel a bigger 'yes,' and every closed door can lead you to an open window. It's about building resilience, learning, and growing from those punches that life throws. In that space between setback and rising again, there's a lesson waiting to be grasped. So next time you face a challenge, I challenge you to look it straight in the eye and ask, "What are you here to teach me?" Embrace it, learn from it, and use it as a stepping stone to crush your next big goal. Remember, it's all part of the beautiful dance of life.

Thirteen

A MELODY FOR THE MAN WHO CHANGED MY LIFE

"From every wound there is a scar, and ever scar tells a story. A story that says, 'I survived.'"
—Patricia Bartell

I spend my first college summer break in Seattle, staying with friends and playing gigs to earn an income. Barbara has made it clear that I'm not welcome on the farm. "You wanted to leave to go live your life, so go, live it," she says. I plan instead to spend the last leg of the holidays with a couple I know from KIOTAC, Dawn and Jim Leonard, in the port-side town of Tacoma. Jim has lined up a gig and arranged studio time for an album I've been recording.

En route to Tacoma, I'm overwhelmed by fear and foreboding. I can't go home. I can't see my family. I'm alone in the car, and I'm crying. There is a familiar pain in my chest, and I cannot shake the feeling that something is wrong. I stop to refill at a gas station, but I struggle to remove the pump nozzle from its holder and insert it securely into the gas tank opening. I'm emotional and frustrated. Behind me, a man's voice says, "No, no, you don't want to do that. Here, let me show you." The voice could be my dad's. I spin around. It's not my dad, but it could be. When Gordon teaches me to do something mechanical on the farm, I often rush and make mistakes in my eagerness to impress him. Now, this man is chuckling and telling me to slow down, just as Daddy would. The echo of my father's voice follows me all the way to Tacoma.

The next morning Jim wakes me up in the early hours. "Patricia, you have a phone call," he says, "It's urgent." Sam, one of my older brothers, is on the line. "It's Daddy," he says, "He's gone."

Gordon had retired from long-haul truck driving a few years back. He had been teaching heavy vehicle operation as part of a vocational certificate program at the tribal Salish Kootenai College in Pablo. He has been fatally crushed by a container in a forklift accident.

"Is Mama there? Is she OK?" is all I can think to ask.

Sam hands the phone to Barbara, who doesn't say a whole lot. Her voice is flat: "You don't need to come home. We'll tell you when the funeral is." There's a long moment of silence. Then I slowly say, "Okay," and we hang up. That's it. I am numb.

I go downstairs to collect my thoughts. Jim comes downstairs later to check on me. I'm supposed to do a concert that night, and I tell him, "I don't think I can perform."

"You need to do it," Jim says. "The music will help you through. Share with the people who have come to listen to you play; they will help bring you through this, too."

I spend most of the day staring dumbly at the wall. I have no words. Far from the family, I'm having difficulty processing it all.

That night, I play a song called The Snow Waltz. Daddy heard me play it for a retirement home. Although he often came to represent the family and offer support, I knew concerts or recitals bored him. He was never effusive or even expressive about my performances. He was just there. And that had to be enough. But that time, he turned to me afterward and said: "Someday, I want you to play that song at my funeral."

So, that night in Tacoma, I play The Snow Waltz. I explain to the audience what had happened and that my dad had chosen this as his funeral song. I try to remain composed as I play, but my eyes sting as tears well and roll down my cheeks. I cannot hide my sadness. And I do not have to. The audience understands loss. As always, the music heals.

I leave five days later for the funeral. My daddy, it turns out, was a popular teacher, loved and admired by his students. They come up to me individually, saying, "Your dad was so proud of you. He always told us how well you were doing and how talented you are." This comes as a surprise to me. I had no idea. I wish he had told me while he was alive.

I have wrapped up the album's recording, but at the eleventh hour, I include one more song, The Snow Waltz. I call the album 'My Best to You,' dedicated to my dad.

WHAT'S DONE IS DONE

Since leaving for college, my ties to the Bartell family have been tenuous: three or four days at the farm for Thanksgiving and a week over Christmas. With my father gone, the bonds are all but broken.

As part of my education degree, I take a course called 'Neglect and Abuse: How to Read the Signs.' On the whiteboard is a bullet point list of the most obvious ones: isolation, skipping meals, frequent bruising, patterns of depression....

"My God," I think, "That was my life."

Gold Nugget

Our past doesn't define us, but it does shape our understanding of the world.

Only now does it dawn on me how bad my upbringing was. You don't know what you don't know. At the time, it was normal, just the way things were.

The course is mandatory as an education major. As a licensed teacher in the State of Washington, I will be legally obligated to report any suspicion of abuse. This is especially relevant for music teachers. Children who are abused are typically afraid to talk. Their voices have been taken away, so they express themselves through music. If you listen closely, they will play their pain for you.

And, for this reason, a music teacher is often the one they confide in and the first point of call when a school is concerned. For the first time, I can look at my past from a different perspective. I now know that what I went through was a million miles from 'normal.'

Each of my adopted siblings has their own story to tell. I do not know their endings any more than I knew our beginnings. We were all rootless lost strands, absorbing what little understanding of life, love, and family we could through passive diffusion, and in different ways, we were all eventually un-anchored.

Cameron had severe learning disabilities but was mechanically gifted and might have made his way in the world. Sunny, Ben, and Amy are all in a care facility or group home. Seth, I think, was returned to his biological mother. I lost contact with John and Daniel. James seems happy now. He has a long-time girlfriend and a blended family. I know he follows me on Facebook. Nicole was always the family favorite. She was six weeks old when she came to us. She clung to Barbara and subsequently received nurturing and attention the rest of us did not. But as Nicole grew up, it became increasingly evident that something was wrong. Sadly, she suffers from schizophrenia and cannot be left alone. Nicole is the only remaining orphan still on the farm with Barbara.

Gold Nugget

Growth is focusing on our future.
Our past is only to show us how far we have come.

Still, in my early 20s, I'm a lifetime of lessons, learnings, magic, and miracles away from the woman I will become, the woman who no longer asks, "What's wrong with me?" The woman with the strength, resilience, work ethic, and sure-footedness to lift little Patricia off the ninth step of the staircase of a house on a farm in the little town of Charlo.

GEMS OF WISDOM FOR CHAMPIONS

The beauty of life is not in never falling but in rising every time we fall.

Pain is inevitable, but so is hope. Both walk hand in hand toward the path of healing.

What's wrong is always there, but so is what's right. Choose what you will focus on, for whatever you focus on expands.

Movement Two

THE SYMPHONY OF LIFE—
EACH NOTE A STORY,
EVERY PAUSE A LESSON.

*"Music gives a soul to the universe,
wings to the mind, flight to the imagination,
and life to everything."*
—Plato

Fourteen

FINDING MY NOTE IN A WORLD OF SKEPTICS

"An artist is not defined by their tools, but by the passion and purpose they bring into their work."
—Patricia Bartell

"*T*his piece is called 'Clarinet Concerto in A Major.' But I want you to think of it as a story. A story about a girl who is lost and can't find her way home. The music is the girl's journey. The notes are like footsteps. They start out lost and confused. And then they get stronger and surer. As you're playing, I want you to imagine you're the girl in the story. You're scared; you're alone. But then you start to find your way. And the music helps you. It gives you hope."*

I'm sitting in a Spokane theater watching *Mr. Holland's Opus*. Just like the evangelist who spoke to me through the TV when I was 15 years old, now Mr. Holland seems to be speaking directly to me. "Find your story in the music, and make the song your own," he says.

It's a short scene in a mainstream movie watched on a weekend with friends and salted popcorn. But it impacts me profoundly.

The idea that I can, without prior permission, insert myself into a piece of music feels as exciting as if I'd trespassed at a museum at night to stand intimately and alone before a public piece of art. The freedom to choose the story Mozart's music tells and to decide how to tell it strikes me as revolutionary and transgressive.

My early home-schooling has embedded in me a belief that there is something fundamentally wrong with my mind and its ability to 'grasp' and 'remember.' Now, Mr. Holland is encouraging me "to imagine," to make up stories, and to think in pictures. This, it dawns on me, is how my mind works: I attach feelings to scenarios. I landmark emotions. I am a creative learner.

Gold Nugget

The journey of finding oneself can be the most beautiful song ever played.

I have been struggling with my own prescribed Mozart for months. I'm uninspired. I don't know how to work it. Frankly, I hate it. But Mozart is a compulsory part of the curriculum, and I have no choice; eventually, I must play it for my instructor. And he is no Glenn Holland.

He has a post-war Eastern European approach to teaching: long on criticism, short on encouragement, and altogether lacking in praise. He stands austerely, with his arms crossed, behind me. He wants me to be cleaner, more precise. He chooses my music; he tells me how to play. He is concerned with accuracy, not imagination. He is worried about my lack of previous technical training. I practice for three to four hours until my fingers ache and my wrists swell. Still, I cannot please him. He tells me that my playing is terrible, that I'll never be as good as his number one student, Larry, and that I'll never make it.

I am working towards a degree that does not yet exist, with a teacher who does not believe in me, on an instrument regarded by academia as a street dog among pedigrees. My accordion and I are on trial for breaking and entry, and my designated defense is having difficulty justifying my right to be there. I think about quitting often.

THE ACCIDENTAL ARTIST

'Imitation is the foundation of all learning, and the best way to become a great artist is first to become a great imitator.'

Aristotle said that, not me. Pre-university, I didn't have access to great thinkers and was not inclined to great thinking myself. But I was an instinctive musician, so I naturally modeled myself on my heroes, like Myron Floren and my teacher, Jim Howerton. I was, in truth, more a mimic than a musician. I copied Myron's physicality, his sound, his every nuance, every gesture, and every detail. If Myron played loud, I played loud; If Myron dropped low, I dropped low. I mostly learned by ear. I had Jim's CDs and listened to them on 'play, pause, and rewind' until his musical expression became mine.

I did not yet recognize the artist in me, but I could hear it in others. And on the day my university piano professor, Dr. Judith Schoeplin, phrases a run of 16 seemingly unexceptional notes so magically it stops me in my tracks, I hear it in her.

"Oh, what did you just do?" I ask.

"What, this?" she asks, flying her fingers across the keyboard.

"Yes, that. Show me how to do that,' I say.

She does it again.

Unlike my instructor on the accordion, Dr. Schoeplin on the piano does deal in artistry. She teaches me how to get the music out of my head and onto the keyboard. She insists I listen to what the music is asking of me. Loud? Soft? Fast? Slow? Joyful? Melancholic? Nostalgic? Enthusiastic? She teaches me the artistry of a crescendo; he just turns up the volume.

But Dr. Schoeplin never does break it down for me in the way that I was expecting, what it is she does so magically on the keyboard. Nor does she explain what I do instinctively. She never says, "That there, which you just did, is a turnaround, a grouping, or a shadowing." We do not explore or take things apart in that way. I find it frustrating because there is so much that I want to learn. I do not want to be an accidental talent. I want to create with intent.

What I'm really asking when she plays those 16 notes is: "Show me how to be an artist."

Gold Nugget

The music of life is not about perfection, but about resonating with the heart.

For that, I need an emotional language I do not yet have. Dr. Schoeplin wants me to understand the piece I play, the history, and the style, and I don't yet know how to ask the right questions or to explain that I'm searching for ways to find my unique expression.

MY DAY 'IN COURT'

My second-year assessment is held on campus in a recital hall with inclining rows of seats around a small stage floor. It's hardly gladiatorial, but I feel like I'm being fed to the lions all the same. The complete music faculty is here, twenty-five or so of them, with their pens and notebooks.

Walking down the steps to the stage, I pass my accordion instructor. He is visibly shaking, clearly feeling the pressure. Close to retirement, after a long and varied career, acknowledgment from the university means a lot to him. His name is on the line too. Perhaps that is why he is harder on me than on his other students. He has been challenged: "We will give you two years; show us what you can do with her." I am, in a way, his last hoorah.

I have a tough audience. "Seriously, the accordion? Come on!" the Choir Director, Mr. Pretty, often playfully says at choir practice. I know others have their own beliefs about the 'grandfather's box' or 'polka box.'

The first piece is a sonata chosen for its technicality and lyricism and because it puts forward a strong argument for the accordion as a classical instrument.

The second piece is called "Toccatina and Fugue" by George Barton. It showcases the accordion's range and depth: A complex interweaving of melody and countermelody from the bass buttons to the right-hand keyboard that creates a hauntingly beautiful harmonic.

Afterward, Mr. Pretty comes to me, "Patricia," he says, "The first piece was ok. But when you played the Toccatina and

Fugue, I threw my hands in the air. My goodness, what can this instrument not play? What can it not do in your hands?"

The voice teacher is floored, too. "Oh, my word, you have these counter harmonies going on, and all these technical things going on, even in your left hand, and it's so beautiful, and..." he gushes.

It's hands-down unanimous: I and my accordion can stay on. We will live to fight another day. And two years later, as a senior, I perform with my accordion at a campus event leading up to our graduation ceremony.

Traditionally, as part of the event, Whitworth University announces the recipients of the Senior Ideals Award. The university annually elects one male and one female senior student for the award based on who best represents the university and what it stands for, and the impact they have had on campus during their four years. I am deeply engaged in university life and proud to have been asked to perform at the event.

In the auditorium, I notice Tom Dodd, my boss at the aquatic center, in a suit and tie. As a swimming coach, I'd only seen him in Polo shirts and jeans. "Wow," I think, "He's sure dressed for the occasion!" We chat briefly. He is fidgety and seems nervous; he tells me he is giving a speech, though he never discloses the subject. I take my seat. A while later, Tom steps up to the stage. I'm listening, but not really; my mind is somewhere else. Then I hear the words, "...one of eighteen children." I sit straight up. "Wait a minute," I think, "Is he talking about me?" Todd continues on about my involvement and influence at Whitworth; he has my full attention now. He explains the significance behind the Ideals Award and how the recipients are nominated and voted in by their fellow students.

The accordion is such an integral part of my passion and identity. Given that its recognition as an instrument worthy of university accreditation has been so tenuous, this award and all it stands for—strong values, commitment, and integrity—belongs as much to my instrument as it does to me.

GEMS OF WISDOM FOR CHAMPIONS

It's not the applause at the end but the journey, the trials, and the growth that make the performance worthwhile.

Embrace your unique story, and never shy away from playing your truth to the world.

In the face of doubt, remember that you are the composer of your destiny, and every note, every decision, counts.

The world is waiting for your song, for your story. It may be different, but that's exactly why it's so essential.

Fifteen

REDISCOVERING MY BOLIVIAN ROOTS

*"In the journey of self-discovery, sometimes the path
we tread leads us to unexpected places and
unfamiliar faces that feel just like home."*
—Patricia Bartell

1999 is the year I return to Bolivia for the first time since my adoption. It's also the year I lose my dad and find my Father.

As a Music Education Major, I must complete a three-week stint teaching at a low-income school or in a foreign country. One day, while traversing the University campus, taking a different route to one of my classes, I see a friend, Coralee

Proctor, in the hall room across from where my class is to be. As we talk briefly, she lights up and says, "You should be in THIS class!"

"Why?" I ask.

"Because you are from Bolivia, and Whitworth University is offering Senior Year students the opportunity to complete the practical part of this class in Bolivia."

I don't believe what I'm hearing. "Bolivia?" I repeat, letting the word roll off my tongue as if trying it on for size.

As always, there are obstacles: I'm only a Junior; it's already two weeks into the academic year, and I don't have a passport.

The staff of Whitworth University rallies around me. Exceptions are made, and I'm granted permission to complete the credit course a year early, so I can slot in and catch up.

I must drive to Helena, Montana's capital city, 320 miles from Spokane and 320 miles back, to apply for copies of my naturalization documents from Citizenship and Immigration Services. Four of my Whitworth guy friends surprise me. They wait for me at my car, dressed like The Blues Brothers, complete with black ties and shades. If I must do a 15-hour return trip, they insist on doing it with me. "We can drive in shifts," they say. So, we speed off, singing at the top of our voices.

I have a friend, Diane van Belle, with long hair to her thighs and the biggest heart, who lives close to campus and goes every day over Christmas break to the post office to check if my passport has arrived.

Everyone knows what this Bolivian journey means to me. My passport eventually arrives the day before my flight, with less than 36 hours to departure.

The trip was sponsored by The Krista Foundation for Global Citizenship, launched by Linda Lawrence Hunt, a professor at Whitworth, in memory of her daughter Krista.

Krista and Krista's husband, Aaron, had gone to Bolivia to serve a three-year commitment in community development with the Mennonite Central Committee, a church organization that sends volunteers to work at the grass-roots level worldwide. In 1998, in something of a tragic South American cliché, Krista was killed on a treacherous mountain pass in an old, overcrowded bus with inadequate brakes, which toppled on a tight turn. Krista was only 25 years old.

Linda Hunt and I both have missing pieces of ourselves buried in Bolivia. It is as if part of my soul has been torn from this country, and part of hers has been interred in it. And although we never meet, the shadow of her grief stretches before me like a noon-day shadow.

But my overriding and immediate feeling is one of anticipation. I am traveling with Coralee, my friend who first told me about the multicultural course and the opportunity to return to the country of my birth. Coralee is as light in laughter and spirit as she is fair in complexion, and we're excited to embark on this adventure together.

FINDING MY TRIBE

The aircraft is headed for Santa Cruz, but we're stopping in La Paz to let some passengers off and others on. Bolivia's capital is situated in a bowl-like depression on the Andes Altiplano, more than 3,600 meters above sea level. The plane descends in what feels like a vertical drop, and the sudden change in pressure causes waves of nausea and lightheadedness. The Bolivians call it 'soroche;' we call it altitude sickness.

It hits me as the doors open. But that is not what takes my breath away. A group of girls are boarding the plane, and it's like looking down a hall of mirrors. They all have my features: dark almond eyes, thick black hair, and brown skin. More passengers follow; I see my face in every one of them.

Growing up, my siblings and I would sometimes play Cowboys and Indians. Because I looked like James and Kenny, I was typecast alongside them as the 'Bad Indian' to the other kids' 'Good Cowboys.' Although I played along, it felt awful to always be on the wrong side of heroism, and I felt lassoed by that old, familiar question, "What's wrong with me?" Here, in Bolivia, there are no "Good Cowboys" to create such otherness. Everyone looks like me.

I've been told that I'm from the northern Aymara tribes, which are taller than the southern Quechua. And were it not for polio, judging by my arm span, I would almost certainly be taller. Still, I look so much like these southern girls on the airplane that yet another layer is added to the many mysteries of my origin. Am I really from the north? Or is my ancestry in the South? Bolivia, it turns out, will raise more questions than it answers.

Gold Nugget

To return to one's roots is to embrace
a puzzle of past and present.

I look Bolivian, but I don't dress Bolivian, I don't act Bolivian, and I don't talk 'Bolivian.' Apart from a few words here and there, 'hola,' 'gracias,' 'como te llamas?' I do not speak Spanish. Coralee, on the other hand, is quite proficient. We make an odd couple. The Bolivian who doesn't know her language, and the blonde-haired, blue-eyed American who does.

Standing in the market, lost in a rail of clothes, I don't notice when a group of women gathers to observe us. Coralee pulls on my arm and says, "Look, they are staring at you." They have come to see this Bolivian woman who speaks fluent English with an American accent. I switch to a Southern drawl and up the volume. The women are befuddled and mesmerized by the incongruity of it all. Coralee is in stitches.

The school where we are volunteering for three weeks is in a poor barrio on the outskirts of Santa Cruz. Bolivians are open-hearted people, and the students and villagers descend on us with great hugs and big kisses. I'm taken aback. I've never experienced such spontaneous warmth or tactile affection. I don't know how to respond. I suddenly feel all too Western, "Oh my goodness," I say, like a lady at the opera who has dropped an ostrich feather from her hat. I'm saved by Chris, a tall, Caucasian, handsome Californian who works at the school. With a wide grin, he pulls me aside and explains, "Patricia, that's how we welcome people around here. You will want to follow suit even if it feels awkward."

I take to these generous acts of affection like a duck to water. So much so that when I first return to university, I run up to a friend, throw my arms around him, and land a big kiss on his cheek. He, of course, has not been initiated into Bolivian greetings. He jumps back, turning beet red. I, realizing my mistake, turn beet red too. Later, on evangelical missions to far-flung corners of the earth, I realize that culture shock is not the confusion we feel when arriving in foreign places but the dislocation we experience when returning home.

Still, after three weeks immersed in a Bolivian way of life, my Spanish is just enough to get me into trouble: I have brought my accordion with me, and to thank the teachers and the kids for taking us into their hearts and lives, I arrange a concert for our final day.

Next to the schoolhouse is a compound. It's no more than a dusty red clearing demarcated by a rusted fence. I've been helping to set out chairs and a makeshift stage with a local teacher, Henry, with whom I've worked these past three weeks. Henry knows exactly three words in English: 'I. love. you.' As always in these tropical lowlands, it's hot and humid, and I'm about to head back to my room for a shower and to practice for the concert. Henry asks me, in Spanish, what songs I've chosen to perform. I start listing the songs I will play, and I'm proud to tell him that one of them is a popular Spanish score the children will recognize. "Besame mucho" I say. He looks at me strangely. I think he hasn't heard, so I lean in and slowly repeat, 'Be-sa-me Mucho.' Henry's eyes dart around the compound, and he shuffles uncomfortably in his seat. I'm perplexed. Until I realize that the song translated means "Kiss me—a lot." When I tell Coralee, she cannot stand for laughing. I don't know who was more embarrassed, me or Henry.

Our jokes paint a thin coat over a sad ambiguity I do not want to acknowledge; beneath the slapstick silliness is an unrequited pleading with these mountains, these rivers, these skies to give back what they've taken from me: my parents, my past.

My field trip to Bolivia gives me a sense of having come from somewhere, a start, an ethnicity. But it doesn't give a resolution. I cannot find a trace of my real mother or father; I cannot find the name or place of the orphanage where I was left at ten months old, and I cannot find a record of my birth.

The night before we leave, I walk around the barrio. I walk down a path and through the open gate of our pension, or boarding house. I take everything in, from the smell of damp soil and frying cuñapé, the chatter of women washing clothes and baby blankets, the giant tropical leaves and the massive tropical bugs, to the relentless call of the katydids. I think, "Well, this is the country I come from, and these are my people." And I know someday I will return to this place and start a school to educate and empower orphaned girls. I know that life will come full circle. But my salvation, it turns out, will not be found in Santa Cruz de Bolivia. It is waiting for me in Boise, Idaho.

GEMS OF WISDOM FOR CHAMPIONS

Sometimes, the answers we seek lie not in the landscapes we explore, but in the hearts we touch along the way.

Embracing our past can pave a golden path to our future, guiding us with lessons and memories.

Life's greatest adventures are those where we discover facets of ourselves, we never knew existed. Embrace the journey, for it will shape and define you in ways you could never imagine.

Let every step you take in your journey of discovery be a dance of joy, a song of hope, and a story that inspires many

Sixteen

WHEN DIVINE MOMENTS DISRUPT THE ORDINARY

"In the midst of seeking, one often finds that the journey and the revelations along the way are the true treasures."
—Patricia Bartell

While my identity is a work in progress, I'm finding my feet on the competition front. Once at university, after turning 18, I graduate from age categories to competing professionally. The stakes are higher, the crowds are bigger, and there's reward and reputation on the line. I'm considered 'the one to beat.'

My performances outside of competitions are getting attention, too. This is brought home to me under the Gazebo in the central plaza in Kimberley, British Columbia. People are dancing around the bandstand, some in dirndl and lederhosen, everyone having fun.

Between artists, the dancers take their seats at their tables or stand to one side, talking. The MC announces the next act: Patricia Bartell. I start. Nobody gets up to dance. Instead, they take out their camcorders and move closer to the gazebo. I smile into a sea of LCD screens. I worry that my tempo is off or my song selection is off, and I will never be invited to play again. "Come on, people, dance," I urge behind my now-frozen smile. Afterward, dismayed, I ask Jim Leonard what happened. "Patricia," he laughs, "Don't you, see? They want to watch you. They've heard about your fast fingers and want to see you in action. You are a phenomenon around here."

My local celebrity status is good for business. In 1997, when I'm 19 years old, I spend spring break with Jim and Dawn Leonard in Tacoma, Washington. Jim helps me record my first album, 'Rivers of Rhythm.' He has a friend with a recording studio near his home and drives me there daily. He also helps me market my music at festivals. The CDs are selling like hotcakes. These sales, combined with the money I'm earning playing private gigs, wedding receptions, bar mitzvahs, and café soirees, and the tuition fees I earn from three private accordion students, give me financial independence.

At the same time, I am loving university life. I'm outgoing, popular, and the life of the party. I'm the president of the women's choir, a part-time receptionist at the aquatic center, and a volunteer at youth groups. I am everywhere. I zip between buildings on my basket-fronted scooter, tooting greetings up and down the pathways. My friends tease that I know almost everybody on campus, and almost everybody knows me. It is almost true.

I am good at masking; I hide a lot. I never speak about my family or my past.

I don't talk about them because I don't know how to explain them. My survival strategy is this: push down and deny. I suppress everything, and inevitably, like an overfilled dam in a deluge, the walls are about to burst.

THE PARTING OF THE SEAS

My dad's unexpected death precipitates a forced entry of emotion. Pain rushes to the surface, bringing with it a residual muck of sorrow, confusion, and fear—flotsam on a river of anguish. My chest hurts constantly. My heart is broken into a million little pieces.

I experience the loss of my father as another abandonment. It's as if he didn't die, but rather as if he left me, just upped and drove away in a long-haul truck on a highway to nowhere. I cannot cope with these unnamed feelings. I become quiet. I withdraw. I am no longer the life of the party, the happiest, friendliest girl in the room. I feel a widening distance between myself and everyone. The sadness rises; I sink.

I don't know which way to turn, who to ask for help, or what kind of help I'm supposed to ask for. In desperation, I reach out to God. Tuesday is worship night on campus; students gather with their musical instruments, sing, pray, and listen to sermons. I still have a skewed view of God in some respects, but deep down, I know He loves me. There is a purity in my love for Him, salvaged from my nine-year-old self, and this offers a portal of hope. I stand at the back of the packed room, eyes closed to everyone's prayers, and call out silently: "Please, God, I need help. Tell me what to do."

The answer comes a few days later in the form of a flyer deposited in my campus post box. It's for a Pentecostal crusade in Boise, Idaho, and the evangelist leading it is the same one who saved me from the depth of depression when I was 15 years old. I know I have to go!

The event is scheduled to take place over three days. I need to fly in on Wednesday and fly out Sunday. But there are mountains to climb: I have my job at The Aquatic Centre on Friday, the Whitworth Women's Choir has its first concert of the year on Saturday, and I'm playing a gig in Portland on Sunday. I don't have enough money for all the flights – Spokane to Boise, Boise to Portland, and Portland back to Spokane. And I have nowhere to stay in Boise. All I know is that I must go.

First, Tom Dodd, at the aquatic center, tells me that the two scheduled practices on Friday have been canceled. "You don't need to be here," he says.

To this day, I'm unsure if the classes were canceled or if Tom simply knew how badly I wanted to go to the crusade. Either way, it was an important lesson in leadership: allowing employees to pursue their passions can ignite their motivation and enthusiasm for their work. Everyone wins.

After Tom gives me the go-ahead, I find out that my three Friday classes are also canceled.

Choir is trickier. I will almost certainly be penalized with a letter grade drop for missing our year's first concert. I meet with Mr. Pretty. I began timidly, "I need to attend this event, and these are the dates…" He is predictably unhappy, "What will I tell the choir that their president is a no-show for their first concert?" He crosses his arms. Although I have never spoken up for myself, there erupts from somewhere deep inside a voice so bold, assertive, firm, and determined that I do not recognize it as my own: "Just tell them it was not your idea," I say. And before my eyes, his whole demeanor changes, "Good answer," he says. "You know, I've always been curious about these kinds of events; I hope it's everything you want and need it to be." He gives me his blessing and sends me on my way. And shouts after me, "Oh, and by the way, I won't drop you a letter grade."

One by one, the obstacles fall away. The organizers of the Portland event offer to pay half my airfare. A girl I know tells me that her parents have two spare bedrooms and will happily host me and my friend, Joe, who has decided to come with me to Boise for the event. Also, her father has taken the week off work for unrelated reasons and is happy to shuttle us to and from the arena daily.

This is what Moses must have felt like at the parting of the Red Sea. There is no turning back now.

BOISE, IDAHO

I see God's grace in Boise. I feel his presence in a way I never imagined possible. I witness the power of collective wonder.

Day One: The doors open to the arena. The music blares. A crowd, fifteen thousand strong, rushes in. Fervor works by contagion. Soon everyone is shouting, praying, and singing in a state of ecstatic worship. Then, seemingly out of nowhere, the evangelist steps onto the stage and joins in worship. As soon as he does so, everything changes. It's no longer words about God in praise; it's now words to God in adoration and worship. Everyone's focus shifts from themselves to a God who loves them.

The atmosphere is electric. People sing in tongues, clap, cry, and raise their hands to Heaven. I have never been in such a setting, but at that moment, I do the same; I lift my arms and close my eyes.

The air seems so dense that I remember thinking these exact words, "the air feels so thick." And then immediately ask myself "Can this be real?" But as I think it, the evangelist says it: "The presence of God is so thick right now..." For the first time, I entertain the idea that God can truly be felt as a tangible presence.

I understand that what I am experiencing is real, that God is real.

I am bathed in liquid love. As if by reverse motion, my broken heart is being pieced into wholeness. I am swept up in the room's energy into the mighty force of faith. I see miracles. There are paralyzed people getting out of wheelchairs, blind people claiming they can see, anxious people luminous with God's love, and everywhere, people in paroxysms of joyful weeping. To me, it is all so beautiful, a magical celebration of God's love. All the while, the evangelist is raising the frequency in the room, leading people, and helping to take their focus off themselves and onto God. "Cast your eyes onto our Creator," he implores. I surrender, and I submit.

I had thought I was broken. I had thought I needed fixing, but right now, I understand there is nothing wrong with me. Amidst this dynamic victory of experience over doctrine, I feel something I have never felt before: real hope and love.

At the start of day two, while waiting for the doors to open, a man I recognize from TV as part of the evangelist's inner circle comes up to me. He asks, "Can I pray for you?" As he does, he tells me, "The hand of God is upon you." I am nine years old again, on the couch with my sisters in the living room, bursting with light and love. I feel something shooting through my body and nearly lose my balance. "Is all that I'm feeling, is this God?" I wonder.

> **Gold Nugget**
>
> *To encounter God is to discover who you really are.*

He grabs me to stop my fall, and as I look at him, he breaks into the biggest of smiles. "God is going to meet with you today," he says.

COMMITMENT

The crusade in Boise changes me. I am fired up; I am hungry to know God in a deeply personal way. I knew much about Him before, but now I can distinguish between a religion about God and a relationship with God. "The truth shall set you free," it says in the Gospel of John, chapter 8, verse 32. I have been freed from the prison of Barbara's beliefs. But what is it that Patricia Bartell believes? What does freedom mean to me? And who is this God that loves me and wants to make me whole?

My upbringing has given me a religious vocabulary: prayer, penance, and deliverance, but what I am searching for is revelatory, not religious. Who am I in God's eyes, and how does this relationship work?

Back in Spokane, every Wednesday and every Sunday, I go to church: the Assemblies of God, Charismatic, Pentecostal, Foursquare, any nondenominational church I can find. I am looking to feel God's tangible presence again. God, of course, is the main topic of conversation in every church I go to. As with a celebrity or a politician on 24-hour cable news, everyone talks about Him, but nobody seems to know Him. Meeting God, I realize, is a spiritual encounter and not a religious rite of passage.

Gold Nugget

Religion is different from a personal relationship with God.

I become a regular at the healing rooms in Spokane, where strangers offer to be a conduit for God. They put hands on me, pray for me, and deliver His messages to me. Not once, not twice, but on three different occasions, I hear, "And He will give you the nations."

I travel from city to city following the ministry and its crusades. Magic happens at these conferences, where the veil between worlds is thinner, vibrations rise, brainwaves slow to an alpha state, and everyone connects without agenda. This is where I meet God, over and over again.

I'm on my own crusade. I volunteer at the book tables, selling the ministry's published works and CDs so that I can serve and be more than just an attendee. I love these big events, the music, the atmosphere of expectancy and hope, and the global resonance of foreign languages as people gather from around the world.

At the end of one crusade, a stranger approaches me. "Hey, I just want to pray for you. Would that be okay?" he asks. "I feel like you don't have a father figure in your life," he explains, "and there's a blessing that fathers pray over their children. So, would you be okay if I stand in place of your father and pray a father's blessing over you now?"

I finally feel alive. I finally feel like things are happening, exciting things. I see signs everywhere, I have encounters and dreams, and I receive downloads in my sleep and in prayer.

In my pursuit of God, much of my life was exciting. However, it did come at a cost. Some of my friends did not understand. Some left me, some criticized me, and others distanced themselves. My friends meant the world to me, so to experience this was crushing, but I wouldn't let up. I could not deny what I had experienced.

It is Tuesday night back on campus, and I'm standing in the back of the room. The worship music begins. I suddenly hear a question in my head that I have come to know as the voice of God. "Are you willing to run the race knowing I have already won it?" Everything in me wanted to say, "Yes, of course!" But I couldn't. Deep down, I know the seriousness of this question, and I only want to commit if I know I will be all in, 100%. I am at 85%. I still have questions. My friend Joe, who accompanied me to Boise and has attended every subsequent crusade with me, together we have experienced tough moments with our friends and families who believe we've 'religiously flipped.' We are sitting in my car and trying to make sense of everything. I have tears rolling down my face. I turn to Joe and ask him, "Is it worth it? Is this pursuit of God worth it? The path sure isn't easy right now." I had many questions and seemingly no one to answer them.

One week later, we are in Phoenix, Arizona. By now, we've developed a sophisticated strategy for getting as close to the stage, to the evangelist, as possible. We know where we want to sit. We know how to time our 'race' once the doors swing open. It's something out of Chariots of Fire. Joe will cut through the crowds and outrun everybody, carrying a jacket to put on the chair beside him.

So here we are to the right of the stage, in the first section of the stadium's bleachers, with a birds-eye view of the entire stage. The evangelist opens his Bible. Suddenly, mid-sentence, he stops and says, "What I am about to teach, only a few of you will truly understand." He proceeds to teach, and to my surprise and shock, he begins to answer, one by one, every question I had asked Joe in the car one week earlier. I'm stunned. Every question I had was being answered. He turns to his right, points in our direction, and with a conviction I'll never forget, says, "It IS worth it!"

I am ready to give God my answer.

The evangelist gestures for us to stand up. He has finished preaching and begins leading us in prayer. But I have my own prayer: "Father, I am willing to run the race. Just one thing, please, never take your Holy Spirit from me. I never again want to venture into anything without knowing you are with me."

I close my eyes to speak personally with God, as I would with a friend, except that there's an authority and security to this 'friend' who answers without words. But face to face with God, my laundry list of wants, wishes, and questions goes out the window; nothing matters because everything and everyone is whole and perfect. I am empty except for massive amounts of love.

Suddenly, the evangelist says, "Touch them so they may know you." Immediately, a bolt of energy hits my body like a vault of electricity through a high-wattage transmitter. I am knocked off my feet. I fall to the floor. I have been 'slain in the Spirit.' Waves and waves of energy flow through my body. I hear singing in the background, "Oh the Glory of His Presence." It is my first encounter with the glory of God. I know He has heard my prayer. It takes all my strength to get up again, and when I do, I know that I am destined for something far beyond myself.

"I am committed," I tell God.

FLY WITH THE EAGLES (OR RUN WITH THE CHICKENS)

My friends are increasingly uncomfortable around me. They want to talk about boys and girls, but I want to talk about God.

At a Bible school, Heart 4 the Nations, I'm introduced to Bruce Allen. Bruce is an acclaimed prophetic with an international ministry of his own and five published works. In time, Bruce will become a cherished friend and close brother, but for now, I invite myself to join him and other ministry leaders from a conference for dinner. I promise not to be a nuisance, to 'just listen,' and not ask too many questions. I want to know what ministers talk about in their off time. Then I remember that I have a friend's birthday party that same night. I'm conflicted. I feel obligated to go to the party. Everything in me wants to go to dinner. Without thinking, I reach for a random book from the shelf and open it. It's by Smith Wigglesworth, and the line that jumps out at me is: "If you want to fly with the eagles, don't run with the chickens." I have my answer.

I've developed what the English poet Robert Bly calls 'an exuberant curiosity in the face of the unknown.' I want to know all I can about God. I am wild with intention, like a storm-tossed tree with roots reaching down for life's great mysteries and branches reaching up toward the sky. I want to fly with the eagles. I join the ministers for dinner.

GEMS OF WISDOM
FOR CHAMPIONS

Amidst the grandeur of miraculous events and life-changing conferences, there often lies a deeper, more intimate message. It's the still, small voice that whispers into the heart, bringing clarity, direction and comfort amidst the chaos.

Uncertainty, questions, and doubts are not signs of weak faith but are the very things that carve our spiritual journey. It is in the pursuit of answers that we find truth. It's the truth that will set you free.

Your pursuit of God is not about the destination but the journey. It's about the intimate moments, the questions, the revelations, and the deep-seated commitment to seek God in every aspect of life. Remember, it's not about how many times you fall but about the strength to rise again, renewed and fortified by faith.

Seventeen

WHEN EVERY NOTE BECOMES A PRAYER

"To sing a wrong note in insignificant; to sing without passion is inexcusable."
—Ludwig van Beethoven

Wherever I find the presence of God, I find worship music. If music can be a bridge between the human and the divine, I reason, a spiritual connection must exist between the musician and God.

The musician has been given a gift, a way to portray the ineffable, and in their notes, we find a path to the holy.

In church, hymns are sung about God; in worship, they are sung to God. Seen this way, all songs become worship music, and playing the accordion becomes my devotional offering.

THE UMBRELLAS OF CHERBOURG

I have been rehearsing a piece called *The Umbrellas of Cherbourg*. It is the opening sequence of a movie of the same name, set in 1950s France. The story follows the love affair between Geneviève, a young salesgirl, and Guy, a mechanic. The film is entirely sung, with dialogue set to music by composer Michel Legrand. The movie's opening shots of rain-slicked streets, deserted alleys, longing, and melancholia are echoed in the mournful strains of the accordion.

But this is not the movie running across my imagination. Instead, this piece becomes a personal time to play for my King. As I practice, it is me worshiping my God through my instrument.

I am performing *The Umbrellas of Cherbourg* at the Bing Crosby Theater in front of my students, teachers, and friends. It's my first performance in a while. I am nervous, and I cannot afford to be. I remind myself that I am not walking out onto the stage alone; God is with me. My heart stills, and my frequency rises. I am inspired. I will play the secret chord to please the Lord.

What happens next is all the more surprising to me because I do not feel at all spiritual in the actual moment of playing. This is long before I've mastered performing under pressure. I'm flooded with adrenaline, and my only thought is to get through the piece without catastrophe. But something special happens, nonetheless.

The next day, I receive a phone call from one of my students. She knows of my spiritual journey. She sounds excited. She tells me of a friend who has been suffering from depression to the point of suicide. My student invited her to my concert to get the friend out of her apartment. After the concert, the friend seemed happy, even elated, and explained that halfway through *The Umbrellas of Cherbourg*, she felt as if a blanket of misery had been lifted from her. "So," enthuses my student, "I just had to phone to tell you because whatever it is you're doing, it's really real!"

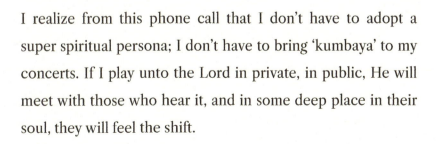

Gold Nugget

True music isn't just heard; it's felt deeply within,
touching the heart of another person.

I realize from this phone call that I don't have to adopt a super spiritual persona; I don't have to bring 'kumbaya' to my concerts. If I play unto the Lord in private, in public, He will meet with those who hear it, and in some deep place in their soul, they will feel the shift.

I started to play the accordion as a little girl to escape my own pain. Now, I play so that others can escape theirs, even if only for the short time it takes to listen to *The Umbrellas of Cherbourg*.

A GEM OF WISDOM FOR CHAMPIONS

The effects of our actions done in private often echo far beyond what we can perceive. Reflect on the positive impacts you've unknowingly made and how you can continue to serve as a light for others.

Eighteen

DISCOVERING FAMILY BEYOND BLOODLINES

"When journeys take us far from the familiar,
it's the shared acts of love that make
anywhere feel like home."
—Patricia Bartell

At a conference in Tumtum on the Long Lake of the Spokane River, Dr. Oniwegbu, a broad Nigerian minister with a big, booming voice, comes up to me as if out of nowhere and says, "Bifor di end of dis year closes out. God 'as a supraiz for yu." And then he walks off.

I first meet Deborah (Debby) Johnston in 2001, not long after my graduation from Whitworth University. At that time, I'm teaching at my accordion instructor's studio, Accordia Nova. I'm twenty-three years old.

Debby's journey to my studio is divinely orchestrated. One day, while rummaging through some records at a second-hand store, she stumbles upon a gospel record she feels drawn to. It features the distinct sound of an accordion. Captivated by its tunes, she plays the record at home, sensing a peculiar urge— she feels she should learn to play the accordion.

That very Sunday, as she leaves her brother's home church, he pauses and tells her, "I really feel you're supposed to learn the accordion." For Debby, this affirmation is all she needs. Immediately, she starts looking for accordion studios in Spokane and soon discovers Accordia Nova. Upon meeting the owner, whom she initially believes will be her teacher, she buys an accordion. To her surprise, the "guru" owner introduces her to me, saying, "This will be your instructor." From expecting a seasoned guru, she finds herself, in her opinion, with a child. And so, lessons begin.

Debby comes religiously every week for her 30-minute lesson and talks almost the entire way through. I learn a lot about her in a short space of time: She is a registered nurse who works in a doctor's practice. She is in her 40s and a devoted Christian. She has seven siblings; they are a close-knit family, and she plays the piano at her brother's home worship services on Sundays. Debby has never been married, has no children, and has always dreamt of having a daughter. Although childless, she is a natural-born nurturer. Many call her "Mom."

I have been warned to maintain a strict teacher-pupil protocol, so I give Debby little back in the way of information about myself. She talks, I listen, and I try to squeeze a practice song in edgewise toward the end of each class. Despite her chatter, Debby advances quickly, and I look forward to seeing her each week. When, after two years, she announces that she is quitting, I am triggered. Abandonment spins me like a legless chair in a tornado, and from the vortex, that old question wraps itself around my chest: 'What is wrong with me?'

Debby cannot give me exact reasons for needing to leave. She tells me she has a strong sense something important is about to happen, and her instinct is to fast, pray, and be still. We speak the same language. I cannot argue with that.

On the upside, I'm no longer bound by the accordion studio's rules of professional conduct, and we are free to become friends. There are very few people, if any, outside the ministry and healing rooms with whom I can share my transformative spiritual encounters, so I deeply value Debby's company.

I spend more and more time at her house and slowly open up to her. I am struggling financially. Students cancel, get sick, go on holiday, don't show up, and forget to pay. I don't know what my income will be from one month to the next. At the same time, the house I share with four roommates is rented in my name. But the roommates are reneging on payments, and I've been left holding the proverbial baby. I'm falling into debt, fast.

"Come live here," says Debby one evening as we clear the dinner table. "Seriously, I have a spare bedroom and would love the company. I won't accept rent because you're like a sister to me, and I would never take money from my sister."

I am too stunned to give an immediate answer.

If you ask, I'll tell you truthfully that I'm reluctant to relinquish my independence. But the real reason I hesitate, the explanation that I would not dare speak out loud, or admit even to myself, is that I am afraid of messing things up. From my experience, the notion of 'family' has always been a deeply ambiguous and troubling one.

That night, I lie awake watching the clock. 10 pm, 10:30 pm, 11 pm, 11:15 pm ... Sometime after midnight, lying on my stomach facing away from the window, I become aware of a bright light to the left of me. I turn to look. It's coming from outside and moving towards me. I focus my eyes, and there, manifested before me, is Jesus Christ. He stands beside my bed, puts his hand on my back, and says, "No longer will you carry the reproach of being an orphan." I did not realize that I still felt like an orphan. A now-familiar wave of love washed over me.

I moved in with Debby on New Year's Eve, the 31st of December 2002, exactly as Dr. Oniwegbu prophesied.

It's the simple things that Debby does that mean so much. On my way out, she calls, "Take a coat. It's cold." I come home and find new clothes spread across my bed. "I saw these today and thought they'd look good on you." Nobody has ever bought me an item of clothing because it 'will look good on me.'

"Do you prefer vanilla or chocolate ice cream?" She asks casually. And I do not know how to choose. Growing up, I was told, "You get what you get, and you don't get upset; you eat what's there and already open." It was unlikely to be ice cream.

Leaving for the airport, on my way to France for an accordion masterclass, Debby says, almost without thinking, "If it's not what you expect, you turn around and come straight home." It has never occurred to me that I have the agency to change my mind or to say 'no' without fear of consequence.

"What color should we paint the walls of your bedroom?" Debby asks. "Lavender," I say, on a random spin of the color wheel. I come home expecting the spare bedroom to be painted lavender. Instead, to my shock, she had completely moved all her items to the spare room and given me her larger bedroom. Who does that? I thought. I'm moved. I hadn't ever had someone show me such kindness and love. The lavender looks awful on the walls. "Can we go back to the original rose?" I ask. "Sure," says Debby.

Self-care, preferences, indulgences, the luxury to make mistakes or change my mind, choice, and a voice. A new world opens to me that is sweet for the expansion it brings, but bitter for the light it casts on what I've missed out on in the past.

Easter arrives. Debby and I go to see The Passion of Christ. It's a beautiful, crisp evening. But on the way home, an old familiar darkness descends upon me. This happens occasionally without warning or seeming reason, a long shadow in a solar eclipse. Debby tries to help me articulate it, but I cannot find the words. When we get home, I go to the couch, and Debby goes to her room. A few minutes later, she reappears and stands before me. "Were you beaten as a child?" she asks. "Yes," I answer. But then quickly follow it up with, "But I'm alright now."

For the next three days, Debby cries non-stop. And I don't know how to make things better. I want to console her, to tell her that I'm OK, that it wasn't all bad, but I do not have the emotional vocabulary. She exits her bedroom in the morning with tears rolling down her face. When she leaves for work, the tears are still rolling. She comes home after work, and her eyes are red and tear stained. I can't take it anymore. I close my bedroom door and pray, "Father, I don't know what to do." And I audibly hear God's voice. As clear as day, He says, "How she cries now, that is how I cried for you." All through my four years at the orphanage; all through the 13 years I spent on the Bartell farm; all through the beatings, the stress, the isolation, the fear, God had been with me, always. I had felt so alone, so abandoned by everything I ever knew. If only I had realized,

He'd been there all along. Finally, I pull myself together. I open my door. Debby opens her door. She looks at me and says, "Whatever that was, it has now been lifted."

In many ways, Debby becomes the earthly expression of God's love that I need to begin healing. She offers: "I'll be a mom to you if you want that?" I think, "I'm 25 years old. I don't need another mom. I already had two, which didn't work out well." But as the weeks go on, I know this is the mom I've always wanted. It's as if she has known me from the beginning. And so, Debby becomes 'Mom,' and I will never have enough words to fully express the gratitude I have for the role she continues to play in my life.

One day, I arrive home from work, and as I pull into the driveway, I see it–and I don't know why I never saw it before. Our house has a white picket fence, and here's Mom, youthful and stylish, approaching from around the corner, and parked alongside my car is her Subaru. It's exactly what I've dreamed of having ever since my early years in Charlo.

MISSIONS: ACTS OF GRATITUDE

Before meeting Debby, I had been on two mission trips: Mexico and Fiji. In Monterrey, Mexico, I told the local people, mostly poor folk living in the slums, of my encounters with God. I played the accordion in worship, showed those who wanted to know how they might hear God's voice, and helped in schoolrooms and wherever else I was needed.

I went to Fiji with Bruce Allen and members of his ministry. I marveled at how far away I was from anything familiar, and that made me ponder the meaning of 'home.' None of my family knew I had left the country. They had all but cut me off. They would never know I'd disappeared if something fatal happened to me. I thought about Barbara and about how a woman could have so many children and not be able to give them the love they so desperately needed. I realized that she had done the best she knew how with the resources she had. You can't give away what you don't have.

Now, traveling on missions with Debby, it feels like I am traveling with all the family I will ever need, and home becomes where the calling takes us.

Gold Nugget
Home is not just a place; it's a feeling of belonging.

We volunteer on an island in the Philippines, where people are so poor that they give us their beds to sleep on, flattened cardboard boxes. Mosquitos maul us, but the islanders' open-hearted love and spontaneous joy was so meaningful.

The poverty in the Philippines is desperate. Our mission aims to introduce the locals to the power of faith in Jesus, but I also want to help in more tangible ways. I ask the islanders what they need most. An outrigger for fishing and transport to and from the island is the unanimous answer.

An outrigger costs $1500, which is more than I have at the time. But I know how to raise it. KIOTAC is only months away. I sign up, and when the time comes, I play as I've never played before; I play as if a life depends on each note, chord, and phrase. I play with purpose and with passion.

Gold Nugget
In a world of uncertainty, purpose fuels passion.

Three months later, I return to the Philippines and purchase the outrigger. Never has winning given me such sustained satisfaction; it teaches me the value of reaching for something bigger than myself.

In Uganda, we work with women who walk all day without shoes across the hot desert to fetch water from half-empty wells. And yet, they give generously of that water so that we can hydrate, wash, brush our teeth, and make ourselves tea. Here, friendships are made instantly and last forever, and acts of kindness are never forgotten. I find it easy to adapt to these places where love is understood on the collective level. And all too hard to return to a culture where smiles and hugs are reserved only for people we know.

Wherever we go, we eat with the locals. Debby has a stronger stomach than me and often tastes the food first. Sometimes, she'll give a subtle brow furrow and an almost imperceptible head shake, code for 'sit this one out.' I feel spoiled. Like a queen whose advisor first tastes her wine to make sure it's not laced with poison. The only time I get sick is when I eat dodgy chicken after a conference in Kampala.

As a nurse, Debby can help these families in more practical ways than I can. They refer to her as Mom and me, by association, as Patricia Johnston, PJ for short. They do not seem to notice that Debby is Caucasian and PJ is Latina. They call me her daughter, and I like the ring of that.

GEMS OF WISDOM FOR CHAMPIONS

No matter where you are or where you go, remember it's the heartbeat of the souls we bond with that makes a place truly resonate as home. It's not about the changing landscapes, but the connections that anchor us. As you navigate through life, crushing it at every turn, let those connections be your guiding force.

Think about it. A simple nod, a heartfelt compliment, or even a spontaneous hug has the strength to shift the universe in that moment. Every single interaction is an opportunity to weave another thread into the intricate quilt of our shared humanity. So, while you're out there conquering the world, remember the immense power your gestures carry.

Every hurdle you face, every act of love you bestow, and every mission you undertake can be that pivotal turning point. It has the spark to reshape your trajectory, redefine your 'why,' and rekindle that burning desire. As you uplift others, you'll uncover an uncharted clarity and purpose in your own incredible journey.

Nineteen

UNLOCKING THE WORLD CHAMPION WITHIN

*"From the classrooms of life
to the stages of the world, every note we play is a
testament to the teachers who believed in us."*
—Patricia Bartell

*D*ebby gives me an emotional language to address my experience. Kendall Feeney translates that language into music.

Kendall is an internationally acclaimed pianist and one of the preeminent performers in the Pacific Northwest. Our introduction is by way of a phone call:

"Is that Patricia Bartell?"

"It is."

"Patricia, I'm seeking an accordionist for a Parisienne Nights concert. I've been phoning around, and yours is the first name everyone suggests. Would you come in for an audition?"

She is a matter-of-fact and to the point. She has the kind of quiet confidence that is comfortable with silences and lapses in conversation. She never speaks verbosely or excitably. She is all grace, composure, talent, and intelligence.

I agree to an audition, and I feel honored when, after playing just one song, Kendall stops me and says, "You're the one we want."

About a year after Parisienne nights, I play at her wedding.

Then, in 2005 I get a call from one of my students: "Do you know about the Taubman technique? Well, Kendall Feeney teaches it!"

The Taubman technique was formulated by a New York musician and pedagogue, Dorothy Taubman, who filmed hundreds of hours of virtuoso piano players. She studied their movements, then devised a method of playing based on arm rotation and keyboard mapping to avoid injury and improve flow and ease of play. Of course, I had heard of the Taubman technique!

I phone Kendall straightaway.

"You teach the Taubman technique?" I ask.

"Yes," says Kendall.

"Will you teach me?" I ask.

"Of course," she says.

And so, in 2005, Kendall Feeney becomes my instructor.

For three months, I play nothing except the C scale. I have a mirror next to me to watch my arm formation. I must relearn how to play from scratch, one note at a time.

I go to Kendall's house once a week. We check in; she watches my hands and arms very closely, then gives me the next set of exercises in the regimen and assigns the next lessons to watch on the Taubman instruction DVD.

Progress is slow and demands more discipline than anything I've ever done. I imagine it's tantamount to a stroke victim relearning to talk. Finally, I play the eighth note. I have had to return to basics to reset my muscle memory. It was worth it. Not only have I finessed my playing, but I can also do runs with an alacrity not previously available to me.

Eventually, the time comes to put it all together. Kendall gives me a piece to play by composer Franz Liszt. Not one given to exaggerated animation, afterward she says, quietly: "You have no idea what you carry inside of you. Your artistry is beautiful." Kendall explains, illustrates, and deconstructs. She encourages experimentation, draws my emotional expression out, and then pushes me further than I've been before.

In the past, in competition, I'd often go to the judges after winning third or second place and ask, "What could I have done better? What can I do to win first place next time?" And they'd inevitably answer, "Oh no, your playing is great." And I'd be frustrated. Kendall gives me tangibles I can work with to be the best.

But mostly, she gives me confidence; she believes in me. There is an expression: 'When you lack self-belief, borrow it.' I borrow mine from Kendall.

I never knew how good I was until Kendall told me. This is why, in 2007, two years after starting lessons with her, I find the courage to put myself on the line. I call her up: "Kendall, I want to compete in the World Championships for accordion, and I want you to prepare me for it."

Kendall is circumspect. "I'm not an accordion teacher," she says.

"But you are a musician," I say, "You understand musicality and artistry. It doesn't matter if it's the voice, the viola, or the cello. You can show me what you want on the piano, and I will adapt it to the accordion."

"Ok," she says, "Let's give it a shot."

From there on, it gets exciting. Although Kendall has the damper pedal on the piano, the artistry she plays with is unmatched. As I listen to her guidance, I see how it can be done on the accordion. She does something interesting on the piano, and I figure out how to achieve the same effect using buttons and bellows. "You can do that on that instrument?" She marvels. It's playful and progressive, a beautiful game of discovery between teacher and student.

This is what I've been wanting ever since Dr. Schoeplin played that magical 16-note run.

Kendall's musical expression feeds my artistry; I have found my unique selling point, my competitive edge. But to brush up on accordion technique, only one man can take me right to the top: Frédéric Deschamps.

I first saw Fred Deschamps at the Coupe Mondiale in London in 2001.

I was 23 years old. I had come to London to see the international competition standard and decide whether I could, should, or would compete at that level. I was intrigued by the technical ability of the competitors but was deterred by the classical, contemporary repertoire that was required at that level. It did not make sense to me. I was, in short, not ready. What caught my attention was a man standing to one side. I noticed the intensity with which he watched the performers. He never took his eyes from their hands, and his body gestures seemed to move with theirs so that I could not tell who was mirroring whom. "Who is that man?" I asked the person next to me. "That's Fred Deschamps," they reply. The Fred Deschamps. The master accordionist and teacher, known in accordion circles worldwide for nurturing world champions.

Six years later, in 2007, at the Maddalena Belfiore International Competition for Female Accordionists in Washington, D.C., I eventually meet Fred in person. He congratulates me on winning third place. "You deserved to win first place," he says. I ask him if he will teach me the chromatic button accordion, as I'd noticed that all the really advanced world championship competitors seem to play this kind of accordion. "Sure," he says, "Come on over to France, and I'll teach you the button accordion."

My intention is to spend two weeks with Fred and two weeks at another accordion school. But I learn so much about Fred's style and technique that I spend the whole month with him instead. It's at Fred's farm that I first meet Grayson Macefield, a multiple World Champion accordionist who competes on the piano accordion. I realize it's not the type of accordion that makes World Champions; it's the artist behind it.

Fred and I discuss the upcoming championships in Italy and the possibility of me competing on the piano accordion. We curate a repertoire that I practice with Kendall when I return to the U.S. Then I fly back to France so that Fred can prepare me for Castelfidardo.

THE WORLD CHAMPIONSHIPS

It takes a metro, two trains, and a bus to get from Charles de Gaulle airport to Frédéric Deschamps' farm in the La Selle-sur-le-Bied commune in the Loiret region of central north France.

Fred offers me his bedroom on the ground floor and takes one of the guest rooms upstairs. The sensitivity of this gesture touches me. There will be no counting steps on Fred's farm.

There are about six to eight students on the farm at any time. We are an international bunch from Russia, Macedonia, Italy, and New Zealand. I am the only American and, not unusually, the only woman. Because of its physicality, the accordion is predominantly a male game.

Our days go like this: wake up, grab a coffee and baguette, lesson with Fred, practice, lunch, practice, dinner, practice, and then the final lesson. It's a long, grueling day. Sometimes, we practice until midnight. At any given hour, the sounds of six to eight accordions fill the farmhouse.

With Kendall, my fingers learned to float. With Fred, they learn to fly. I work harder than I've ever worked before. I must. I'm swimming in the big sea now as amongst our group are some of the best accordionists in the world.

Then, a week before the competition, disaster strikes.

I am playing my full program for Fred, and we realize that my repertoire is a song short. "Oops," says Fred in his very French way. "Oops," I say. This, of course, is a euphemism tantamount to a surgeon's "oops" when the scalpel slips. I think, "This is bad, really bad." Fred hands me a new sheet of music. It's a piece he taught me on the chromatic button accordion. Still, it might as well have been a new piece since all the hand positions and the landscape of the runs are completely different on a piano accordion versus a chromatic button accordion.

"You've got one week to learn this," he says.

Playing a song on the accordion takes muscle memory. Your fingers work faster than your mind, and your right and left hands simultaneously perform different functions at different speeds. Like changing gears on the car, if you overthink it then everything seizes up. Fred comes past my practice room often. "Sl-oh-w-her," he says, "Go sl-oh-w-her." In music slow is a four-letter word. To learn fast, you must practice 'slow.'

A musician hears a song in their head and immediately wants to play what they hear. But the body must be trained; muscle movements must be programmed into cellular memory. The discipline is to play 'slow' until you've mastered the technique. Only then comes the artistry and the speed.

The time for 'slow' is now. But I am running out of time.

The days speed by. Six. Five. Four... Three days before the competition, I'm having a one-on-one lesson with Fred. He sits on the couch by the fire, and I sit opposite him. The Russian, Petar, comes in from his practice and plops down alongside Fred.

He listens to my struggle with the new piece.

He looks at Fred. "Fred?" he asks, "Are you sure?"

"Oui," Fred answers.

"But it's like three days away," says Petar.

"She's up for ze challenge, so I am up for ze challenge," returns Fred.

And I'm thinking, "Well, if Fred sees it as a challenge, that means he thinks I at least have a chance..."

The day before we leave, I can finally play the whole score. I'm still missing one or two chords. I'm not happy with it, but it's what I've got.

ALL THE WORLD'S A STAGE

We pile into Fred's horsebox truck. I sit up front with Fred, and the guys sit on benches with our luggage and accordion cases in the back. And off we go, speeding down the country roads, careening around corners. We fly on JetBlue to Italy, hire a car, and make our way to Castelfidardo, the accordion capital of Italy and host of the 2007 Castelfidardo International Championships.

Castelfidardo is off the beaten tourist path in Italy's Marche region. The overland journey from the airport takes us through a patchwork of vineyards and golden fields stitched together by lines of cypress trees. The town is comprised of ancient cobblestone squares, narrow streets, colorful facades, and terracotta roofs. Sheets are drying on balconies amidst flowerpots. The incantation of 'nonas' exchanging recipes mixes with the recital of prayers in town churches. At night, people sit in side-street cafes drinking Verdicchio. One gets the feeling little has changed in Castelfidardo for centuries.

It's been decades since an American has competed here. We Americans have a bad reputation for underestimating the accordion and are thought to lack the technical breadth and emotional depth of our European counterparts. What's more, the entire panel of judges are men. I am not just an American, I'm an American and a woman, and one who walks with crutches, at that. I am, for all intents and purposes, an outsider among outsiders. But I am studying with the maestro, a world-renowned teacher who wins world titles. So, I have everyone's attention.

Fred comes to my hotel room to fetch me. I am wearing a full-length black dress; my hair is freshly blow-dried, and I have my game face on. I am armed with lip gloss, my glamorous black gold and white Pigini accordion, and all the courage I can summon.

For all my polish and professionalism, I am nervous. For the first time, I cannot think of what to say to Fred, and we cross the square in silence. We enter a small building, ascend the elevator, and walk into a crowded room with only standing space remaining for the audience still making their way in. I shuffle past the judge's table, a row of stern-looking, cross-armed men frowning in concentration. Someone announces my name: "Patricia Bartell from the United States of America." I walk to the front of the room and position myself; Fred hands me the Pigini and gives me a wink that says, "It's all up to you now."

I start with three big chords, "Boom Boom Ba" I miss my first Bellow change. I must recalibrate. In music, as in business and life, it's not the mistake you make; it's what you do next that matters. At this level, you can leave nothing to chance. I have lots of re-starting points memorized. If I get in a bind, I jump seamlessly to the next start. I'm prepared. I look at Fred; he gives me a small, reassuring smile.

Gold Nugget

The world's stages are vast and varied, but every performer knows: the true competition lies within.

I make it into round two. We're down to five contestants in my category.

The second round includes the new piece. In competition, any weakness is amplified, and I'm not as confident as I'd like. I miss the first leap. And the second, and I look over at Fred. He shifts the weight of his body in an exaggerated shoulder drop. I readjust my shoulder; it's a micro movement that yields big results. I don't miss another leap, and from there on, it's plain sailing.

The award ceremony is a gala event. I have on black pants and a black jacket with silver sparkles. The MC speaks Italian, and I don't understand what he says. I do not speak any Italian, and I'm distracted and fidgety. Then Fred leans over and tells me, "You're in the top three; time to go backstage and collect your world championship title." I just make it into the wings as the MC announces, "In third place, Patricia Bartell from the United States of America."

First and second place went to Fred's students, the Russian and the Italian, respectively. But I feel as if I've won gold. I am 29 and reached the podium of one of the accordion world's most esteemed competitions. From Charlo, Montana to Castelfidardo, Italy via the school of hard knocks. Not bad for a farm girl on crutches.

CALL IT BY ITS NAME

I am excited to share my success with Kendall. This victory is as much hers as it is mine. As a keepsake, I have brought two wine glasses imprinted with 'Castelfidardo, October 2007' and our names. I pass the gift to Kendall; she smiles weakly. "Patricia, I've been diagnosed with colon cancer," she says.

She is only 48 years old. My chest hurts.

Kendall lives ten more years with cancer. During that time, we start an Argentine Tango Quartet called Tango Volcado, joined by Euguene Jablonsky on bass and Tana Bland on violin. Eugene is Spokane's go-to bassist. He has played everything from chamber music in European palaces to country hits in backroad wild west honky-tonks. Tana Bland is a member of the Spokane Symphony and frequently tours with Broadway productions. Both are exceptional talents. But Tango Volcado is so much more than the sum of its parts. On stage, we have an electric camaraderie; off stage, we push each other to take risks and explore new musical territories.

At our first rehearsal, Kendall leans over and says, "Let's be clear; here we are, colleagues. Here, I'm not your teacher." And so, a new dynamic develops between us.

Kendall speaks little of her suffering or the disease slowly eating away at her. But pain softens her. Once, I visit her in bed, and she takes my hand in an uncharacteristic show of vulnerability. We sit like that in silence. We have gone from a teacher-student relationship to being colleagues in a band to being co-creators of a course: "The Art of Musical Expression."

Another time, towards 'the end,' after a rehearsal session, I walk out with Kendall after the others have left. In the front yard, she drops to her knees. In a barely audible voice, she says, "Patricia, I want to live. I still have so much to do. Patricia, who will even remember I was here?" I get down on the grass next to her. "Kendall," I say, "me and all your students. You will continue through us. We are your legacy."

Gold Nugget

Legacy is not just about being remembered, but in the lives we've touched and transformed.

The last time I see her, she is unconscious, heavily dosed on morphine. Her husband leaves the room so that I can say goodbye. It's as if I am 14 years old again, standing alongside Kenny's body. But this time, I have language. This time, I can call Grief by its name.

GEMS OF WISDOM FOR CHAMPIONS

With every note I strike and every move I make, I feel the impact of those who've touched my heart. They leave imprints, like melodies and rhythms, that shape our path. Dive deep and ask, "Whose song is playing in the background of your heartbeats?"

There's an art to bouncing back. Each time we lift ourselves, each moment we stand tall after being knocked down, we're not just moving on; we're crafting a powerful chorus in the song of our existence. Remember, your life's song is composed not in the quiet moments, but in the bold declaration of, "I will rise again!"

In this grand performance called life, each of us is more than just a player, we are Champions. Our lives, the highs and lows, the tears and the triumphs, don't just create solo performances. Together, we are co-creating a magnificent symphony, interwoven with tales of struggles, triumphs, and profound connections. Celebrate each melody, for it's a chapter in the story of us.

Twenty

AN ORPHAN'S PATH
TO THE GLOBAL
STAGE

"The melody of life isn't defined by where you start,
but by the crescendos you achieve along the way."
—Patricia Bartell

There are three Accordion World Championships: Coupe Mondiale, Trophée Mondial De L'accordéon, and the Castelfidardo International Competition. Fred Deschamps is president of the Trophée Mondial De L'accordéon. After the competition, he sits on the couch listening to my latest CD, turns to me, and asks, "What do you want to do with your music career?" I answer, "I want to be the best teacher I can be."

"What else?" he asks.

I wasn't sure what he was getting at. He proceeds to tell me: "Patricia," he says," I need someone with your integrity and artistry on the panel of adjudicators for Trophée Mondial De L'accordéon.

Accepting this position means Castelfidardo will be the only World Championship I compete in. Fred gives me time to deliberate. I don't need to think too hard. I am 29 years old; I have been competing since I was 12, and it's time to move on.

At the championships, each adjudicator is called by their country, Mr. Germany, Mr. Italy, Mr. France, etc. Of course, my claim to fame is: "Miss USA." But Fred has given me the nickname "Princess" because he explains, "You are super lovely and delicate, musically and humanely." The name catches on, and among the adjudicators backstage, that's what I'm affectionately called: Princess.

Over the next decade, I will crisscross the globe from Sarajevo, Bosnia, to Albufeira, Portugal, to Vigo, Spain, to Pineto, Italy, to Kunas, Lithuania, and back to Portimão in Portugal, as an adjudicator for the Trophée Mondial De L'accordéon. But in 2012, I'm appointed President of the USA World Trophy Accordion Organization, and Fred suggests I host the Trophée Mondial De L'accordéon in Spokane.

It's a first for the United States. "You just need to book a few rooms at the hotel in front of ze venue," he says. Of course, he doesn't realize the enormity of the undertaking as in Europe, governments help fund these kinds of events; not so in America. My students and their families pitch in to help. This would be one of the biggest events we'd ever host. We have a jam-packed schedule, from fundraisers to concerts. At least 12 to 15 judges are on every panel for each category. There are 16 countries represented among competitors. Participants from every country, the best of the best, will fly into the Spokane Airport, ready to vie for the coveted world trophy.

Meanwhile, as I listen to the Spokane Symphony rehearsing, it hits me that this is no daydream; it's reality. I had meticulously played out every detail of this event in my mind, and now here I am, with tears welling up behind my eyes because, finally, it's unfolding before me.

The weight of responsibility and the immense stress, known only to my mom and me, has burdened me for months. From the financial costs to delivering an authentic American experience for our international guests, the pressure is immense. Despite all our fundraising efforts, we fell short of covering even 50% of the event's expenses. Nevertheless, with the combined proceeds from ticket sales and program book sales, I can write the last check, pay off the last hotel, and settle the outstanding balances in full. We break even! And against all odds, the event is a resounding success.

Our team takes charge, warmly welcoming competitors from the airport and ensuring a smooth transition to their hotels. I book the judges into Spokane's high-end historic Davenport hotel and arrange transportation to and from the venue. I organize traditional American fare: hamburgers and French fries, a swing band, a children's choir performing a song specially written for the event, and beautifully designed programs. The mayor of Spokane gives the inaugural speech; the symphony performs on opening night. There is a flag ceremony representing each participating country. I have a network of over 60 volunteers and group captains. The local media - print, TV, and KPBX Radio - are all present. It's an extravaganza.

That same year, Whitworth University honors me with an Alumni Award for the graduate who has achieved the most in the shortest time. I am thirty-four years old. But what I consider my greatest professional achievement comes three years later.

On Monday, the 11th of May, 2015, Spokane's daily broadsheet, The Spokesman-Review, publishes the following article written by local journalist Lenny Lapidus:

"Accordionist Patricia Bartell sweeps symphony with solo.

Two of the brightest planets in Spokane's musical firmament teamed up this weekend when accordionist Patricia Bartell joined Eckart Preu and the Spokane Symphony Orchestra on the stage of the Martin Woldson Theater at the Fox.

Bartell's appearance onstage brought the audience immediately to its feet and occasioned a burst of whistling and shouting unusual in that auditorium. The Spokane musician is plainly a star, and the reasons are not hard to find. The mastery of her instrument is absolute, which enables her to use the accordion as a resonator for her soul, reaching across the gap between her and her listeners to make their thoughts and feelings vibrate in tune with hers...

In a pre-concert conversation with Preu, she attempted to explain her ability to make her instrument sing like a human voice as a function of manipulating the bellows and vibrating the keys on her Hohner. You might as well try learning to fly by watching a bird.

...The audience did not want Bartell to leave the stage without an encore, which she graciously supplied with an improvisation so brilliant that one felt that the whole orchestra was still playing."

I had, for two consecutive nights, performed Astor Piazzolla's concerto, Aconcagua, alongside the Spokane Symphony. Aconcagua is the highest peak in the Western Hemisphere. It represents the height of Piazzolla's career. And the height of mine.

Gold Nugget

Summits aren't just mountains; sometimes, they're moments.

I had dreamt of this occasion. The full sound of the orchestra at my back, Debby in the front row, Kendall next to her. (It is the last time Kendall would see me perform.) And beyond them, my students.

When the music started its final ascent, I imagined I was at the foot of God's mountain, climbing to meet him. This was my Aconcagua, but it was also my Hallelujah. As the orchestra began its ascent, as the piano joined in, and then the strings, and the cello, and the brass, and the timpani, all building to a crescendo, I felt awe at His power.

Gold Nugget

From the world's rejection to God's affection, through the language of melodies.

This was the point to which God had brought me: from a malnourished, neglected child crawling on an orphanage's dusty floor to the summit of Aconcagua, with the full weight of the symphony to support me; and my friends giving me a standing ovation.

God had taken what the world did not want and, by my testimony, created a witness to His love.

GEMS OF WISDOM
FOR CHAMPIONS

Every soul carries its own 'Aconcagua'—a peak moment waiting in the embrace of time. For some, it's the electrifying applause of a crowd; for others, it's that profound whisper of self-realization in solitude. My symphony stage was not just about music; it was a crescendo of sweat, tears, and relentless spirit. What's your crescendo?

Dive deep within. Pinpoint that defining 'Aconcagua' moment in your journey of life. How has it sculpted you, and more importantly, how will you amplify its power to shape your tomorrow? When I'm facing a challenge, I relive my 'Aconcagua' moment and in that state, I make the decisions I need to solve the challenge.

From the shadows of an orphanage to the limelight of a symphony stage, my journey isn't just about grit or gift, but a melody of divine love and grace. You hold a symphony within, a story that can inspire a world waiting in anticipation. Sing your song and share your journey because your voice has the power to ignite a universe.

Movement Three

ADVERSITY DOESN'T DICTATE OUR STORY; IT'S OUR RESPONSE THAT SHAPES THE CHAPTERS.

"The mediocre teacher tells. The good teacher explains. The superior teacher demonstrates. The great teacher inspires."
—William Arthur Ward

Twenty-One

CULTIVATING BOTH SIDES OF THE MUSICAL BRAIN

"Teaching music is less about notes and more about the hearbeats between them."
—Patricia Bartell

*S*hinichi Suzuki, the developer of the Suzuki method for music, which teaches children to play music by ear, once said, "Teaching music is not my main purpose. I want to make good citizens. If children hear fine music from the day of their birth and learn to play it, they develop sensitivity, discipline, and endurance. They get a beautiful heart."

Pablo Casals, the world-renowned cellist and conductor, called music "The divine way to tell poetic things to the heart." And neurologist Oliver Sacks called it "A remedy, a tonic, orange juice for the ear." There is not a known culture of which music is not part, for as far back as our species can be tracked, and there is something deeply profound about that.

As music teachers, we do no more, no less, than provide our students with a way of understanding the human experience.

In 2001, after graduation, I take over all my accordion instructor's students and take on an additional part-time job at Northwest Christian Elementary School, teaching classroom music from kindergarten through grade two.

I am ORFF level one certified as well. The ORFF music method, developed by composer Carl Orff, is premised on the belief that every child has natural musical abilities, and that learning music should be a joyful experience. In ORFF music classes, children use percussion instruments like drums, xylophones, and tambourines to create rhythms and melodies. They also get to sing and move their bodies to the music. The ORFF method focuses on making music fun. And fun is what we have!

There are about 22 to 24 students in a class. As one class files out one door, another class files in through a second door. Three mornings a week, there's a jolly conveyor belt of 274 enthusiastic learners in and out of my music room.

I have an intuitive understanding of the different ways these children work. I read them: the introverts, the extroverts, the logical thinkers, the storytellers, the creatives. I give the more creative thinkers the drums to play as they usually have an ear for the baseline beat. I give the more analytical thinkers triangles as they approach rhythm rationally and logically with the left brain.

Gold Nugget

Different strengths, equal talents.

Ultimately, music is a whole-brain activity but as different students walk through the different doors, I know which door to lead them through.

After two years, I feel it's time to resign my tenure. The headmaster understands I have missions to serve, a business to build, and a music career to pursue. But I'm not allowed to tell the children that I'll be leaving until the final day. So, I arrange a concert with the theme of a king, and I make each child a flag. I sit up late at night cutting, gluing, and pasting 274 flags. On one side of the flag, it says: 'Jesus loves you.' On the other side, it says: 'So does Miss Bartell.'

When my final day at Northwest Christian Elementary arrives, the principal announces in assembly: "Today's Miss Bartell's last day with us, and we want to thank her, and…" Unprompted, the kindergarteners and then the first graders, followed by the second graders, shuffle down the bleachers towards me, many in tears, to hug me.

It's hard being the one who leaves.

Part of what makes me popular with the children, I believe, is that I remember all too well what it's like to be a child. I remember watching Myron Floren on television: I felt happy when I played happy. Music rescued and transformed me; I want it to do the same for them.

The children talk to me with music in ways they won't with words. I know how to listen. They don't realize it, but every chord tells its own story. Music is a language; the notes are words, and once you know what they mean, you can understand what is being said. I know how to interpret their messages. And so, I can meet the children where they're at.

I'm not really in the music business. I'm in the business of unleashing 'beautiful hearts.'

Three months after leaving Northwest Christian Elementary, I'm in the mall when someone behind me calls, "Miss Bartell! Miss Bartell!" I turn around. It's one of my little boys from Northwest Christian Elementary. He runs and hugs me. His mom catches up to us and tells me: "Brian came home from school on the last day of term and refused to speak for days. We didn't know what had happened. Finally exasperated, I just sat on the floor next to him and said, 'You know, honey, I'm here to help you. What's going on?' And he mumbled: 'Miss Bartell left.'"

THE RED B LINE

Around the same time that I leave the elementary school, the accordion studio is sold. The new owners intend to keep the previous owner's legacy alive, but they have no mind for the business, and the school is not growing. It's time for me to branch out. I phone Ron at Music City and inquire about renting a room. He tells me to come talk to him.

Music City is a converted funeral home. The entrance is still lined with its original red carpets and fake flowers. Baby grand pianos stand along the passageway like well-attired butlers waiting on *The Last Waltz*. Ron rents out upstairs rooms to music teachers, and the sounds of students practicing piano escape beneath closed doors and half-mast windows.

"What do I have to do to get you in here? Like, tomorrow. I'll have someone help you move your piano, and you can take my office on the ground floor. I'll move up to the first floor," enthuses Ron.

I move into Music City and register Able to Play Music, LLC. It's 2003, I'm 25 years old and a licensed business owner.

One of my first new students is a little nine-year-old girl. She is blond, bubbly, and petite with bright, clear blue eyes. This is her tenth lesson. She sits on the bench and puts her music on the stand. I start by casually checking in on how the week went.

"Did you practice?" I ask. She freezes.

"Is everything okay?" I ask.

"I couldn't practice," she tells me in a small voice.

I open the book, and she confesses, "I can't remember the first note."

We had gone over it many times in previous lessons.

She looks at me with a question in her eyes that I am all too familiar with. And I am seven years old again, staring at the phonetic symbols in my exercise book, unable to recall what vowel sounds I'm supposed to make. In those bright, clear, and beautiful eyes, I read the question behind her question. "What is wrong with me?" This little girl thinks she is stupid, and that breaks my heart.

Why is it, I ask myself, that some children learn to read music with such ease while others struggle? Why could James recite all the Mayflower dates by heart, and I couldn't remember any? I want to understand everything I can about how the brain works. And I want to find a way to help this little girl.

I wake up one morning from a dream about the "Red B Line." This dream inspires the basis of my method of reading music. The music staff has 5 black lines, and on, above, or below those black lines are dots signifying which note on the instrument to play. The brain comprehends in chunks, but 5 lines are too much for the creative brain. In my dream, the middle line is red, making reading the notes easy. Now, my creative students only have to see two lower black lines, two upper black lines, and in the middle, a red line where note B lives (for the treble clef), hence the name, the Red B Line. Now, they have a mental picture.

I don't want creative children with big hearts and wild imaginations to give up on the technical demands of sheet music.

One day, my colleague, Ron Lento, comes flying down the stairs, stops at my music room, and says, "Patricia, you're gonna love this! I have discovered a new Australian piano method called "Simply Music." He begins to tell me about the program. It resonates immediately.

While I am formulating my "Red B Line" system to make reading music easier for my students, Neil Moore has patented a method that bypasses sheet music altogether. This 'play first, read later' approach is grounded in the belief that everyone, without exception, is naturally musical.

Moore, an Australian-born musician based in Sacramento, California, draws an analogy to how we learn a language: speaking before reading and writing. With Simply Music, the student builds a musical vocabulary, learning chords, rhythms, and patterns by first learning a song in its entirety and then progressively breaking it down to understand its components. It is akin to learning a sentence before learning individual words. In this way, reading is delayed until students have already fallen in love with music and their own creative expression of it.

Moore's Simply Music curriculum is for students like my little blond-haired, blue-eyed girl. The black and white notations and fractions of notes and chords and rhythm mean nothing to her. She thinks in color, emotion, and story.

So, I switch the curriculum to play to her strengths. We start with one of Moore's Simply Music compositions: 'Night Storm.' "What kind of storm is it?" I ask her. "Is it way out there over the sea and slowly rolling towards you? Is it soft at first? Does it get louder, louder, and louder as it gets closer? Is it a scary storm?" Now she is in the story, creating the story, expressing what she sees and feels. And once she is immersed in the music, she can hook the notes and chords to her feelings. There is nothing wrong with her mind. As it turns out, this little girl, who could not play the first note, is a beautiful musician and a magnificent storyteller.

I have another student who is brilliant beyond brilliant. At 9 years old, he has an encyclopedic knowledge of antiquities and architecture. Reading music comes easily to him; he has the technical makings of a champion. I tell his parents, "Start saving now because he will need a high-end instrument. He is going to go fast."

But this little boy has high-functioning autism spectrum disorder. He struggles to read facial expressions, social cues or to identify even basic emotions: happy, sad, or angry, in himself and others. He cannot connect to the music. And in his emotional muteness, I again see myself: A little girl mimicking Myron Floren because she intuits that if she can play 'happy,' she can feel 'happy.'

This boy has an analytical, logical mind. For him, the storm cannot be soft, loud, scary, or reaching a crescendo. I can call out instructions in piano-speak: forte, fortissimo, fortississimo. He will tell you what these words mean: "loud, very loud, as loud as possible," but for him, they have no correlating sounds. For him, the storm must be measured. So, I create a logic-based system using a metric on a scale of 1 to 12, with 1 being the softest and 12 the loudest. I tell him, "Start me on a 5, build to a 10, and end on a 12," and he will play a storm rolling in forte, fortissimo, fortississimo.

Bit by bit, using other parts of my new system, I see my logical students fall in love with music, and I see my creative students fall in love with music. It works. Using the same principles, I even expand it to the next level of reading and playing rhythm.

Different strengths, equal talents. The goal is the same, but the door through which they step is different: I must encourage artistry in the logical thinker and build technicality in the creative. I must bring the two hemispheres together and allow the music to do its magic.

Gold Nugget

Music: where logic meets emotion, and both find harmony.

(Watch my TEDx Talk on YouTube:

"Rethink The Way We Teach Music")

My hope is that by the time they are done studying with me, they are so well-balanced that they will thrive personally. On stage, an untrained ear will not know which is the left-brained thinker or the right-brained thinker. They will have the whole package. When these children enter competitions, other teachers comment: "You always get the talented ones."

SIMPLY MUSIC

One day a 12-year-old girl enters my music room and starts playing quite a complicated piece. I am listening to her, but I'm also watching her. In the physicality of playing the accordion, the body cannot lie.

I ask her how she is, and she responds politely, "I am fine, thank you." I don't think she is fine. I think she is sad, very, very sad. This pre-teen has a strong personality with formidable intelligence. She is articulate and a fast learner; she is on the school debating team. But the way she strikes the keys and pulls the bellows tells another story. She puts her heart and soul into the song. I watch her, and I think, "What must her interior life be like? There is such desolation in the way she plays."

And I am again a little girl, curled up on the 9th step of the staircase.

I cannot step in uninvited. I cannot pry about her home life. What I can do is help her to tell a different story. I show her that the song could mean something else, that there is perhaps another way to play it. And so, we begin to craft a new narrative through the music, one that will make her feel more positive.

"Change what you see, and what you see changes."

I see myself in each one of my students. But now I have the tools to heal them. And in doing so, I heal the broken parts of me.

Twenty-Two

HOW THE ACCORDION DEFIED ITS OBSCURE PAST

"Just as music adapts and evolves, so should our methods of teaching, ensuring relevance and passion for aspiring students."
—Patricia Bartell

The accordion finds its place in the realm of American melodies in the late 19th and early 20th centuries. It accompanies waves of immigrants from Italy, Germany, and Poland who arrive with empty pockets and accordions in their cases.

It provides the bittersweet soundtrack to homelands lost and a homeland found: In the tenderness of its timbre, it acts as an anchor for close-knit immigrant communities looking to bridge the Old World and the New. Like alien vegetation, diverse, persistent, and transformative, it adapts to the popular rhythms of jazz and swing and becomes a staple of speakeasies in the 20s and 30s. But it reached its zenith in America in the post-war era, as the Silent Generation waltzed into forgetting through polkas and dance halls, hungry for prosperity.

Then, in the 1960s, the accordion lost its footing, side-lined by the counterculture, and overshadowed by the electric guitar with its amplified sound and spirit of rebellion. By the 1970s, it has been relegated to reruns of *The Lawrence Welk Show* watched mostly by middle Americans with an average age demographic somewhere between 'Retired' and 'Dead.'

In the 80s, the accordion keeps a modicum of cool by starring in iconic songs, like Leonard Cohen's *Dance Me to the End of Love* ("Oh let me see your beauty when the witnesses are gone.")

In the 90s, rock stars like Bruce Springsteen, with his American anthems underscoring the working class's struggles, keep their sound alive.

In the 2000s, rock, indie, and folk fusion bands like Mumford & Sons introduced a new global audience to the accordion. But in each decade, for each of these artists, the accordion is no more than a subtle sound effect.

Now, in 2010, Gilbert Reyes believes that the world is ready to revisit the accordion as a center-stage instrument. Gilbert is the brand manager for Hohner in America. Hohner, founded in 1857, and headquartered in Germany, is one of the largest and most highly regarded manufacturers of high-quality harmonicas and accordions worldwide.

Gilbert wants to deepen Hohner's inroads into the American market and capture a new market. But his passion goes beyond the dictates of his job. He wants to preserve and promote the rich tapestry of music that our instrument brings to life. And he believes that the time for an accordion renaissance is now. The advent of digital platforms is allowing niche genres and artists more visibility and the opportunity to reach wider audiences. Social media facilitates forming communities centered around specific interests and musical styles. Accordion enthusiasts, musicians, and fans can connect, share performances, and promote their music through dedicated online groups and networks.

FRAME YOUR VISION

It's January 2010, and I have just returned from a mission trip to Entebbe, Uganda when I receive a call from Gilbert. He introduces himself and proceeds to ask many questions about accordion education in America and my own methods specifically. We have an immediate affinity, bound by our Latino roots and love for the accordion. But unlike Gilbert, I have never located myself within the grand sweep of the accordion's narrative. I am simply a musician, preoccupied with teaching my students and building my fledgling business in Spokane. I have never considered myself a frontrunner or a pioneer. Gilbert gives me a new perspective.

Gilbert has heard that my studio has one of the largest teen and young adult demographics among accordion schools across America. Students travel in a 360-mile radius from Montana, Canada, and Oregon to take lessons with me.

It is not uncommon to have young students who are initially reluctant or indifferent sent for lessons by enthusiastic parents. It's most common to have elderly students returning to 'learn accordion' because it's on their bucket list. It's most unusual to have so many teenagers who willingly and autonomously choose to play accordion. My students do.

I have put together a modernized accordion band called The Portatos. It is a musical ensemble (comprising about a dozen members) that incorporates the accordion, violin, bass, and percussion with contemporary elements and often includes choreography, showmanship, and sometimes visual media. Yev and Corrie, who came to me as 17- and 18-year-old students, front The Portatos.

The Portatos have a more modernized playlist. My students want to play music they can relate to, contemporary songs like *The Final Countdown*, expressive genres like Tango Nuevo, and songs with big themes and little riffs they can pour their hearts into.

Gold Nugget

When words failed me, the accordion spoke;
its bellows breathed the emotions I couldn't voice.

The accordion gets a poor rap because it's poorly played in America. And it's poorly played because it is generally poorly taught. Many accordion players are self-taught. Gilbert tells me that any attempt to restore the accordion to the popularity of its '50s heyday must take a grassroots approach. It must start with the way a new generation of musicians is educated. The market must be tilled, turned, and seeded. And Gilbert believes that I am just the farm girl to do it.

Gilbert and I discuss developing a curriculum and making a Hohner-certified program. We would look at many options for it. Meanwhile, I need a curriculum for students that is easily accessible 24/7. AccordionLifeAcademy.com is born. It encompasses my method for making music easier to read, my spin on what I have learned from Kendall Feeney on the Taubman Technique and from Fred Deschamps, my search for artistry, and my discoveries on left-brain/right-brain activity. It will cover everything from sheet music to how to hold an accordion, from posture, arm positioning, and which fingers play, which bass buttons to depress, how to pull the bellows, how to play the keys, music theory, and more. It is a mammoth undertaking.

The outcome is a fully-fledged core curriculum, with a series of short instructional videos covering each level, a separate bass course, and stand-alone technique training with Fred Deschamps.

AccordionLifeAcademy.com has an online community, weekly group Zoom sessions for students, an online shop selling instruments, accessories and sheet music, and a stand-alone digital magazine called *Accordion Life Today*, all based on a subscription model.

But it takes a decade of development before AccordionLifeAcademy.com reaches maturity, and in the immediate future, I intend to leverage the beauty and efficacy of Neil Moore's Simply Music for my absolute beginners.

I must complete the in-depth teacher's course and the entire student program to become a licensed Simply Music practitioner. The estimated time for certification is six months. I take one week off work to become certified. During that time, I listen to Neil Moore for so many hours each day that I start developing an Australian twang: "When a musician's improvisin', they're really creatin' spontaneously a series of notes and organizin' 'em in a way that makes sense...."

The deeper I go into Simply Music, the more I am convinced I've got to make this available to my accordion students. It's made for piano, but it wouldn't take too much to modify it for the accordion since the right-hand keyboard is already a piano keyboard. So, I reach out to him by email, not really expecting an answer. After so many hours and days immersed in his wisdom and the beauty of the Simply Music program, the man has become something of an icon to me.

Two days later, the phone rings. I am a little awestruck and so used to listening to his recorded voice that I sometimes forget to answer his questions. He is as warm, energetic, and eloquent on the phone as he is in his filmed lessons. At the end of the conversation, he suggests, "Patricia, instead of using the existing program, why don't we create a whole new program: Simply Music for Accordion." I bring in Gilbert and rope in Fred. But I am the face of Simply Music for Accordion.

There are 18 levels to Simply Music, from Beginner to Expert; we will concentrate only on the first four, aimed at beginners who have never learned to read music. For me, the magic lies in those early stages, allowing students to play something sophisticated from lesson one and fall in love with a language before studying its grammar.

Twenty-Three

UNLEASHING THE VOICE THROUGH CAMERA CHARISMA

"Life is not just about finding your voice; it's about letting it be heard."
—Patricia Bartell

As the face of Simply Music Accordion, I need to shoot dozens of instructional videos, each highlighting a different lesson for a different skill level. Before we start shooting, Neil suggests I fly to Sacramento to make a promo video in which he'll interview me about the program.

Some weeks later, he is in Spokane for a masterclass collaboration with Fred Deschamps and me. Neil cannot wait

227

to show me the uploaded and edited promo. He takes out his tablet, clicks the link, and presses play. His enthusiasm is contagious. "The video just went live on YouTube!" he says.

I watch the screen; he watches me. And when he sees my face, his demeanor changes. He says kindly, "We can make it un-live if you want?" I look at Neil and say, "I know I can do better than that!" He understands. I don't know how at that moment, but I know his brand deserves better than I've just seen on his screen.

I first saw myself on camera as a teenager at the Kimberley Old Time International Accordion Competition. Someone had filmed me walking up the six stairs to the big green stage, walking across the stage, taking my seat, performing, and walking off the stage at the end of my performance. "Do you wanna see it?" they asked. "Sure," I answered, "why not." I was utterly taken aback by what I saw. Now I understood why people asked me, "What's wrong with you?"

Now, I was asking it of myself. "Who was this, swinging her crutches awkwardly up the stairs? Who was this girl with leg braces and a graceless gait?" I didn't like the way she walked. I didn't like the way she looked. "What was wrong with her?" Until then, I believed my accordion allowed me to shine. Suddenly, it became a subterfuge. I wanted to hide behind it.

I have those same thoughts now. Here is a woman of indeterminate age, seemingly terrified, in an ill-fitting gray jacket and shoulder-length permed hair, with a timid voice and almost no expression. I don't like the way she looks, and I don't like the way she talks. "What's wrong with me?" I ask myself.

Gold Nugget

From self-doubt to spotlight just by
changing my limiting question.
(Watch my TEDx Talk on Youtube:
"What's Wrong With Me: Redefine Your Crutches")

That night, I use the hours of precipitated insomnia to Google 'media training + online presentation skills.' There are several. I settle on one called JV Media. I fill out an application, and two days later, I receive a callback. I'm told the producer of the company will do my training. He has read my application, teaching the accordion on camera. He is intrigued and challenged. He also happens to be a producer on the NBC Today Show. The day course requires flying to Chicago for six hours of training. I'm told if one has never had camera training, they need an eight-hour session; if one has had some training, a six-hour session. I negotiate four hours as that's all I can afford. I will have to learn fast.

Professional musicians, like professional actors, learn early in their careers that 'if the mind can visualize it; the body can mirror it.' The same applies to presenting, which really is a form of acting. But while my musical training gives me a head-start, using my voice is an unfamiliar, foreign experience.

At first, I feel ridiculous. Worse, I feel triggered. Growing up, we were never allowed to talk back or offer an opinion out of turn. And certainly, we could not raise our voices, not in animation nor in anger. Children are meant to be 'seen and not heard.' What was said: "Speak when spoken to." What was demanded: "Do not offend. Do not anger. Do not object. So do not ask questions. Never say no."

The realization that my voice had been taken from me, figuratively and literally, comes as an unwelcome epiphany. "Louder," repeats the producer. "Even louder," he encourages. To me, it sounds as if I'm practically shouting, but this is what the camera wants. My voice echoes in my ears. It is as if I'm hearing it for the first time. Patricia Bartell is speaking up!

Voice training and gestures are only two of the components we cover in the training. We also touch on style and presentation. A lady so flawlessly groomed she looks like a photoshopped version of herself goes through the dos and don'ts of makeup and what to wear on camera. She has been a newscaster for 24 years.

Growing up on a farm in Montana, my wardrobe was comprised of hand-me-downs, work boots, and oversized shirts. Anything outside of that had to be sewn by me. I had a red handkerchief 'special occasion' dress I made myself. I wore it with a wide black belt with an enormous buckle and topped it off with a Stetson hat. I must have been a sight to behold! In the Bartell home, fashion was never given any thought or attention.

Modesty was the only requirement. I had a lot to learn.

Before flying to Chicago, I am asked by the Producer, "Are those curls real?"

"No," I say sheepishly.

"Permed hair looks lifeless on camera," he explains.

So, back home, I tell Debby I need a new style. She knows of a high-end precision cutter, Nelson, and books me in. I've never heard of a precision cutter before. It turns out to be someone so skilled and expert with scissors that no matter what you do, your hair always falls back to its primary position. Such skill does not come cheap. As I sit in his chair, Nelson circles me, lifting my hair here and there. Finally, he says, "This is what I recommend: Cut off the curls. Your hair has a beautiful sheen to it, and that's what you want the camera to pick up. If I cut the curls off, your hair will be about three inches long. But I suspect it grows fast." Personally, I like my curly hair, but I'm also ready to move on. So I tell him to go ahead and do it quickly before I change my mind.

Gold Nugget
Sometimes, change demands more than just a new perspective; it demands a new look.

He takes a curl right in front of my eyes and "snip." There's no going back now.

I'm in my Toyota Highlander, barely out of the parking lot from getting my curls cut off, when I get a phone call from the Producer in Chicago. "Have you cut your hair yet?" he asks. "I have," I confirm, looking in the mirror as I answer. It's true; every hair is in the same place the stylist left it. I think the cost of his precision has stunned my follicles into obedience.

I leave Chicago armed with some universal basics: styling tips, applying makeup for the camera, a crash course in body language, and how to project on camera. Most importantly, I leave with confidence. Little did I know that four short hours and one expensive haircut would butterfly-effect my career. Years later, in a way that, with hindsight, makes divine and destined sense, "Present, Persuade, and Profit on Camera and on Stage" will become one of the cornerstones of my business offerings and the unique selling point of my brand.

We shoot the videos. Gilbert, Neil, and I fly to Germany to present Simply Music for Accordion at Hohner Headquarters. They give their endorsement and blessing, and we launch the program at Trophée Mondial De L'accordéon in Spokane in 2012.

Twenty-Four

THE SILENT STRUGGLES OF A BUSINESS DREAM

"It's often through the cracks of our plans that the brightest rays of opportunity shine through."
—*Patricia Bartell*

During the Trophée Mondial De L'accordéon in Spokane, I am approached by a friend who says there is a businessman called Lulu who would like to meet with me. He has a property for rent that he thinks would work well as a music studio. I now have over 40 students across piano and accordion and two student teachers. I know that we have outgrown Music City. Lulu and I meet over dinner. He is a small-built, kind, and delightful Frenchman with white hair and a 4,000 square foot, three-story, turn-of-the-century, brick-faced building for rent.

Lulu takes me to see the building. Cobwebbed relics from the twenties and thirties are piled floor to ceiling, and paint peels from the dilapidated walls. But I have a vision. Bash a wall down here, add a reception desk there, a lick of paint, and a bit of imagination, and we'll have a studio. I take it.

My students are excited about the move. Everyone pitches in; we roll up our sleeves and spend a weekend transforming the abandoned building into our new home away from home.

Fast forward ten years, and visitors enter the building into a small atrium with mailboxes. Then, they walk through two high-security metal doors. (The back of the building houses fiber optic wires and a database large enough to power the whole of downtown Spokane. It has nothing to do with my academy.) The metal doors open into a long hallway.

To the right is our front office and waiting room with a tea and coffee station and hot chocolate or apple cider, depending on the season. There is always background music. Parents and children sit on large comfortable sofas talking or doing homework. A smart screen is mounted on the wall with slides announcing upcoming events. Behind the reception desk, where students sign in, is our logo.

On the hour, or half hour, the doors open, and teachers come out followed by their students. The hallway erupts into a hive of activity, greetings, jostling, high fives, and fun. The reception fills with parents and children coming and going. Then suddenly, it goes quiet. Until the next changing of the guard. In the afternoons, you can hear the bands practicing: drum rolls, a bellows tremor, a guitar strum, a piano run, a bass beat, a roar of laughter, and a spontaneous song.

People come for the music; they stay for the community.

By 2022 I have 245 students, 12 teachers, and two bands. This is the house that I envisioned, and now here it is. But there was a time when that house almost came falling down.

DARKEST BEFORE THE DAWN

Soon after moving into our new premises, I am approached by one of the international adjudicators on the panel of Trophée Mondial De L'accordéon. He wants to move to America and is looking for a salaried teaching job at the studio. I know him to be a teacher of the highest order, but I do not think my fledgling school has space for two master teachers. My every instinct is to say, 'no,' which I do several times. He is persistent. "Come on, Patricia, let me help you build this thing. We can do it together," he promises.

My main reservation is my students. The music room is a sacred space. Students reveal much about themselves through their play; they allow themselves to be courageously vulnerable. So, the music teacher-student relationship must be built on trust. I will have to convince them that this new teacher can successfully take my place while I take on a more administrative and business development role.

My students are willing to give him a chance. So, several months after our first meeting, I give in. Overriding my instincts will prove to be an expensive mistake (but also a gift in disguise).

As an abandoned and poorly treated child, I trusted nobody. As a liberated university student, I trusted everybody. As a businesswoman, I will eventually learn to find the medium.

While the new international teacher takes over my students, he fails to bring in new business. The first month's payroll comes along; I sit at my desk, signing checks and trying to convince myself: "This was a good idea, wasn't it?"

By the second month's payroll, I ask myself, "Was this a mistake?" The studio is hemorrhaging. The international judge is bleeding us dry.

I pace the long hallway, asking myself: "How can I make it work? How can I make it work? Can I make it work?"

I am madly advertising, distributing flyers on car window shields and in post-boxes, placing classified advertisements in local newspapers, on postcards on notice boards, and mining prospects through third-party mailing list providers. Nothing. I'm like an anachronistic newspaper boy looking for dimes and missing the dollars. I've heard of digital marketing but do not know what it means. I'm a musician, not a marketer. I had spent years crafting my skill but knew nothing about business, accounting, or marketing.

After several months, I meet with Mr. International in the office to review my notes on his students. I make my points. He listens. And when I've finished, he says, "I want to thank you for everything ... and goodbye." His wife had won the green card lottery, and they were up and moving to her family in Florida. He never had any intention of building anything. He has been biding his time and using his proof of salary to stay in the US until immigration approved his residency. My students are happy to come back to me, but at the same time, we've all been burned.

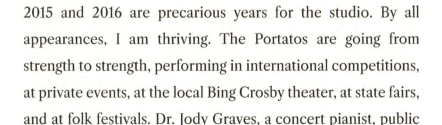

Gold Nugget

When one door closes, sometimes it's not about finding another door, but creating one.

2015 and 2016 are precarious years for the studio. By all appearances, I am thriving. The Portatos are going from strength to strength, performing in international competitions, at private events, at the local Bing Crosby theater, at state fairs, and at folk festivals. Dr. Jody Graves, a concert pianist, public speaker, and former cultural ambassador for the U.S. State

Department in the Middle East regions, joins Tango Volcado. I reach my peak as a guest artist with the Spokane Symphony. And AccordionLifeAcademy.com goes live.

But none of it is adding to the bottom line. The balance sheet is still skewed to the right. Although the judge's departure means I'm no longer paying his salary, I am teaching again, which means I'm spreading myself thin. We're a slowly sinking ship.

I take time out to have lunch with a dear friend of mine, Dr.Elizabeth Welty. I first met Dr. Welty while teaching at Accordia-Nova. Many of my students felt like outcasts, lonely, or let down by their friends and peers at school. Remembering all too well what it was like to be home-schooled and friendless, I created for them a makeshift family of sorts, a band of seven, 9- to 15-year-olds called The Accordia Nova Diamonds. The kids met once or twice a week to rehearse. The studio was their place of belonging. Being in a band taught them to make music in collaboration rather than competition. They cheered when one of their band family excelled and empathized with their disappointments. And because they were having fun, they improved dramatically in a short space of time.

When Elizabeth Welty called to say she was looking for musicians for an annual fundraising event for the Spokane Symphony, I agreed to perform but suggested that the Accordia Nova Diamonds perform, too. "Great! Bring them in," she said. It was their first major show.

The fundraiser was called Christmas Tree Elegance. It was held at the Davenport Hotel. We went all out. I found a seamstress to make the girls white satin gowns. The boys wore tuxedos. The kids loved every minute of it. So did their parents. For Elizabeth and me, it was the start of a beautiful friendship.

WHERE THERE'S A WILL, THERE'S A WAY

Elizabeth Welty is a feisty, engaged nonagenarian, a retired physician inducted into the Spokane Citizens Hall of Fame for contributing to local arts institutions. She once told the press: "I don't play an instrument nor paint. A real knowledgeable person I am not. So, you see, I am always an observer, always in the audience." But as Anne Pratchett's fictional Russian ambassador says in *Bel Canto*, "It's a kind of talent itself, to be an audience." Elizabeth Welty is an exceptional audience.

Although she was already 90 years old when we first met, we had lunch together once every two to three months for almost a decade. She just loves listening to how the studio is doing, what missions I've been on, where in the world I've been adjudicating, and what conferences I've been to. "Your life should be made into a movie," she often says. Dr. Welty has a vested interest in my school and the well-being of the children; she provides several scholarships for children whose parents cannot afford the tuition fees.

But by 2016, she is frail, almost blind, and partly deaf, and I do not have the heart to tell her that the studio is hanging on by a thread. She must have heard it in my voice, though, because halfway through lunch, she leans over, puts her paper-thin hand on mine, and says, "Patricia, everything is going to be OK. You'll see. Everything will be fine."

I didn't know it at the time, but this is to be our last luncheon. A few days later, before she can attend the Northwest Bach Festival, Dr. Welty falls out of bed. She has always said that being so short, little, and close to the ground, she will never have to worry about falling. It is the only thing I ever known her to be wrong about. The fall aggravates a back injury, and after that, she fades fast. She is transferred to a senior frail care facility, and I last see her four days before she passes away in September 2016. She was one hundred and one years old.

In the following weeks, I try to console myself with her words, "Everything will be OK," but I am barely covering my overhead, I'm not drawing a salary, and I'm feeling desperate. I sit up at night googling 'business courses,' 'marketing courses,' and 'how to grow your business.' I then shift from Google to Facebook, where I begin to scroll mindlessly. Suddenly, Facebook shows me an ad, "World Class Marketing." I think to myself, that's exactly what I need. I click the advertisement; it sends me to a landing page where everything I read feels like it was written just for me. I click the registration link, fill out the information … and am then greeted with the investment, $10K. "Must be a typo," I think at first. I don't even have USD $100 to my name. I leave the registration incomplete.

Late the following night, after trying to balance the books again, I walk down the academy hallway, peering into empty rooms, switching off lights, collecting forgotten objects for lost property, and tidying the coffee station. The day's energy coats the stillness, like a glass lake after the chaos of wind and its wakes retire. I stand in the reception room with a heavy heart. If I do not do something soon, the doors will have to close. I am on the brink of losing everything I have worked so hard to build.

The next morning, I woke up with a new resolve, "I will find a way. I will attend 'World Class Marketing.' I just don't yet know how..."

Two weeks later, as I'm running out to a rehearsal, an official-looking brown manilla envelope is delivered to my door. I have been waiting for sheet music to arrive in the mail, and I assume this is it. I flip it over, and my heart skips a beat. This is not my music. It's from a lawyer's office! I tear open the envelope and scan the document. Have I forgotten to pay a bill? Have I broken the law? Is someone suing me? The blood rushes to my head.

I restart the letter several times before I see a small, attached note that says, "It's not much, but it will help," signed, "Dr. Elizabeth Welty." In her will, she has left me enough to attend the "World Class Marketing," Business Mastery with Tony Robbins.

On the other side of a crisis lies opportunity. What I thought was a mistake—hiring Mr. International—turns out to be a gift in disguise because a new world is about to open to me, one that will take me down a widening path I never could have imagined existed.

Movement Four

**BUSINESS ISN'T JUST TRANSACTIONS;
IT'S A SERIES OF CHAPTERS THAT
CHRONICLE RISK, RESILIENCE, AND
RELENTLESS PURSUIT OF VISION.**

*"You are not fool's gold, shining only under a
particular light. Whomever you become, whatever
you make yourself into, that is who you always
were. It was always in you."*
—Tara Westover, *Educated*

Twenty-Five

FROM FLIGHT DELAYS TO SIX-FIGURE DAYS

"In business, patience isn't passive waiting; it's active preparation."
—Patricia Bartell

I am on a United Airlines airbus homeward bound from Chicago, wedged between two businessmen. From the misted, rain-slicked windows, it's difficult to judge the distance from the tarmac to the runway. We are in limbo on the taxiway. We have been this way for hours, and the mood among the passengers has moved from frustration through resignation to restlessness and settled on agitation.

It's Friday afternoon, the 20th of May, 2022. At 2 p.m. the next day, I am scheduled to go live with the most important

245

masterclass I've ever given. The promise is: "Discover the High Ticket Structure and How to Design, Launch and Sell Your Product or Service in a way people want to buy." It is, in fact, a meta masterclass. I will be selling my own skill-based service by showing other people how they can do the same.

In the reflexive world of high-ticket mentoring, we call this a Six-Figure Day. I will have four hours to shift mindsets about money and remove objections that keep clients spinning in circles in their businesses. In the end, they can clearly make a decision to either run with the content I teach and do it on their own or do what they already want to do, and that is to join my program. A percentage will join my program, and that will push me into the 100k-earning bracket. In so doing, I will prove to be 'the product of my product.'

I have already proven my methods with private clients in different niches. I enjoy growing other people's businesses. Now, it was time to do it for me.

One hundred and eighty-six people have signed up for my masterclass. One of my own mentors has agreed to join two hours into the event to do a 'pre-pitch' warm-up to my closing. (It's a one-in-a-million opportunity I can't afford to miss.) My fellow mastermind members are waiting to see if I can pull this off.

There are moments when all the things you've done, all the things that have been done to you, and all the things you've yet to do converge. They stop running beneath and before you, and they become you. This is one such moment.

These four hours will be a snapshot of all I've learned, all the mistakes I've made, and all the success I've gleaned on the way to becoming an entrepreneur, the owner of a six-figure scalable academy, and a business mentor. It's been a winding road that started in the dark, empty hallway of my music studio on the brink of losing everything I'd worked so hard to build.

But the clock is ticking. The storm is raging. The wind is blustering. It seems as if everything is moving except our airplane.

The man to my left has switched out his connecting flights five times in as many hours. The only outlet for his anxiety is to pick up his phone every two minutes as if Siri might find a way to stop the storm. I fear he might have a cardiac event.

The man to my right is as calm as if on a docked yacht in the middle of the Mediterranean Sea on a warm summer's day. He's making jokes and laughing at his own humor.

All we can do, really, is sit, wait, and watch. We watch Alaska Airlines take off, Delta, and every other airline. "I'm being very conservative," admits our polite pilot over the PA system, "but your safety comes first."

"Of all the flights I've been on, did today have to be the day I get the most cautious captain in American skies?" laughs the man on my right. The man to my left glares at him.

It strikes me that I have been placed in this seat at this time to remember one of life's most important lessons: We cannot control what happens to us, but we can control how we respond. Attitude is always a choice. I choose to go the way of 'the man in the Mediterranean.' I surrender.

I have just spent two days in Chicago for a photoshoot. I was scheduled to return on the red-eye to Spokane on Saturday morning. On Thursday evening, I receive a notification from United Airlines: "Storm warnings in Denver: 90% chance of cancellation or long delays." (Denver is where I catch my connecting flight.) I cannot risk missing my own masterclass. At the eleventh hour, I am rerouted through Salt Lake City, but my new flight leaves Friday afternoon. I must wrap up the shoot early and race from the studio to the airport.

Friday is a beautiful day, sunny and unusually windless for Chicago. The shoot runs like clockwork. My wardrobe has been expertly curated; the photographer manipulates the lighting and cleverly positions me for just the right balance of authority and accessibility. My crutches are positioned as if they were the six-foot legs of a supermodel. My hair is blow-dried, and my face is professionally painted. The weather, however, is less compliant and impossible to control. On route to the airport, the sun disappears. By the time I check in, storm clouds have gathered. By the time I board, the heavens have opened.

"Disruption always follows intentions," one of my mentors tells me. Today is a case in point.

After six hours on the taxiway and another hour on the runway, the pilot sees a gap. "We have a three-minute window," he announces. "Fasten your seatbelts and prepare for takeoff." Again, I'm struck by the allegorical nature of this weather-hijacked flight.

In the realm of business, windows of opportunity may be chance occurrences; but it is the astute entrepreneur who recognizes the opening, seizes it, and transforms it into a gateway to success. Rewards come to those who are willing to act decisively. It's a balancing act of patience and urgency.

Gold Nugget

Opportunities in business don't always knock twice.
The trick is in recognizing them, even when they appear
in the guise of adversity.

I have been patient. This is urgent.

To launch this masterclass, I've had to step outside my comfort zone, defy conventional wisdom, and trust my instincts. I want to show my clients that they don't need to wait to package their offering perfectly but that they can go live without a huge social media following, without even an email list. I lead by example; I have pulled it together in under two weeks.

> **Gold Nugget**
>
> *Showcasing and demonstrating your expertise provides a credibility that signals you walk the talk.*

I intend to demonstrate the power of a live performance, so I have posted just one pre-masterclass invitation:

"Not sure where to start with creating and launching a high ticket program? Or maybe you're not sure how to package it so that it warrants a high ticket price and a price that you feel good about? Or maybe you're wondering, 'Where do I find people who will even buy it?' and then how to sell it to them in a way that would be an easy 'yes' for them without using slimy high-pressure manipulative sales tactics that are a complete turn-off. If you would like a simple five-step path to create and launch your high-ticket program, I have a solution for you. I'm Patricia Bartell, and in my upcoming free masterclass intensive, I'll share the model I used to design, launch, and sell high-ticket programs. And if that's what you're looking for, you're in the right place..."

A presentation is a form of performance. As a musician, I have been performing competitively since I was twelve years old. And whether it's music or money, the notes are the same: pitch, tone, and timing. You take your audience on an emotional journey, obliterate objections, connect, and hold their attention. This time, however, I've made promises. Everything's on the line.

Gold Nugget

While logic might make people think, emotion is what drives them to act. People will only do what they "feel" like doing.

We escape through the three-minute window. The storm breaks, and I return home in the early hours of Saturday morning. There are other obstacles: the WIFI connection is unstable, and my computer crashes. I still have the words looping through my mind: "Disruption always follows intention." But at one minute to two, the background music plays, and the countdown starts four, three, two... "Hello Everyone! How many of you are truly ready to step into the next level for your business, into your destiny, into your purpose? Wave at me if you're ready to make a shift from stuck to unstuck, from scattered to scalable, or from broke to being the best in your field. If that is you, type YES in the chat for me!"

It's in these moments of uncertainty that true innovation and growth occur. I met my 100k mark twofold, with twice the anticipated conversion rate.

Gold Nugget

Success isn't achieved overnight but is the accumulation of years of trials, tribulations, learning, and refining.

Afterward, a colleague says, "It's unbelievable that you achieved all that in just four hours." I elaborate: "Four hours plus five years and a lifetime of learning."

GEMS OF WISDOM FOR CHAMPIONS

Onlookers see the four-hour performance; only the artist knows the years of preparation that led to it.

Every entrepreneur will face storms—moments where everything seems against them. But it's the unshakable belief in your mission that will carry you through. Ask yourself: Is my belief in my purpose stronger than any challenge I face?

Your greatest lessons aren't found in the calm but in the midst of chaos. The storm isn't your enemy; it's your classroom. In the midst of these events ask, "What is this challenge teaching me about myself and my business?"

Two people. One storm. Two realities. Understand that your perception is the lens through which you see the world and determine your reality. Do you see storms as setbacks or setups for greater breakthroughs?

In every disruption, there's a hidden door to a greater dimension of success. It's not about waiting for the storm to pass but learning to dance in the rain. Are you looking for doors or are you fixated on walls?

Every intention to rise will be met with winds of disruption. The stronger the wind, the higher the potential ascent.

Massive success isn't about massive action. It's about improving 1% every day, taking one more step, pushing one step beyond your limit. Over time, that 1% compounds into unstoppable momentum. Where can you add that 1% more effort today?

Let these insights guide you, empower you, and remind you of the titan within, waiting to emerge. Let's "Crush It" together.

Twenty-Six

CONFRONTING BUSINESS FEARS HEAD-ON

"To find success, first find yourself."
—Patricia Bartell

On the 17th of August 2017, I stand in the lobby of a Las Vegas hotel collecting my entry tag to Tony Robbins Business Mastery. The queues to register are long. I check the time on my Apple watch (a birthday gift from Debby). Behind me in the line is a young lawyer; we get chatting. He, too, is checking his Apple watch. Surrounding me are professionals of all ages and all walks of life. Many of them are suited and booted for business; many of them are wearing Apple watches. During handshakes, the watches slide out from under jacket sleeves like revelations of a secret code. I have a strong feeling that I've found my tribe.

The double doors open at 8 a.m. sharp. We take our seats. The atmosphere is already electric with anticipation, but when Tony Robbins walks out onto the stage, the ante rises to supercharged. The music blares and 2,500 people get to their feet, shouting and whooping in welcome. The song belting through the speakers is "Life will never be the same again" by L' me Immortelle. Little do I know that it will become an anchor and an anthem to the transformation after transformation I'm about to undergo.

Everything about Tony Robbins is supersized: his booming, gravelly voice, his six-foot 270-pound frame, his smile, and his charm. When he spreads his arm in an encompassing embrace, he has the wingspan of a golden eagle. When he claps his giant hands, the displaced energy reaches all four corners of the room. When he punches the air in victory, it's as if Zeus himself is commanding lightning to part the heavens.

Tony Robbins uses his words very intentionally. His movements, stories, tonalities, and humor purposefully aim to do one thing: expose and challenge the belief systems that hold us back.

I have watched the Netflix documentary on him, *I Am Not Your Guru*. I have researched this man that Forbes calls the CEO whisperer; who has coached almost every US president since Clinton, mega-celebrities, golf champions, and UFC fighters; who has built a multi-billion-dollar empire starting as an overweight kid with an empty stomach and an appetite for achievement.

Despite the documentary's title, Tony Robbins appears to be a secular evangelist, lifting the energy in the room and presenting a new way of thinking. "Business is a game," he says, "and once you know the rules, the rest is all strategy." But I soon discover there is only one thing that comes in the way of a business owner and their success: Themselves.

I had studied the scriptures found in Mark 12:33, but I had missed two keywords, "To love Him with all your heart, with all your understanding, and with all your strength, and to love your neighbor as YOURSELF..." In Boise, I met God. Here, I meet myself.

In the crusades, we are guided to take attention off ourselves and onto God. Here, the attention is drawn to the center of our self, to the core of what motivates us. "The *how* will come; you just need a *what* and a *why* that is bigger than you," Tony says, stretching his arms to their full seven-meter wingspan. Business, we're told, is 20 percent mechanics and 80 percent psychology."

I know nothing about psychology. My quest to know God has led me to an understanding of spirit. But I have no language for the science of the mind. I have never identified the filters through which I make sense of the world; until this moment, I was unaware that such filters even existed.

The epiphanies roll in like waves of thunder in an electric storm.

One idea punches me in the gut: "When you realize that you are the bottleneck, you can start to break through your limiting beliefs and take massive action to create the results you desire." I am the bottleneck. The proposition that I am all that stands between me and business success is both terrifying and exhilarating; terrifying because of the extent of my subconscious programming, growing up muted, shut down, and numbed. Exhilarating because change is in my control. I have the power to overcome my limiting beliefs. What Patricia *chooses* to think is going to determine what happens next.

I watch as 'the suits' let go of their armor: ties loosen, jackets come off, and shirts are untucked. The Apple watches are whooping for their lives. And just as I did in Boise, I throw my hands in the air and join in. Then it was in the greeting of God; this time, it's in getting to know thyself.

We are all open, raw, and ready for change. I am fully immersed, taking it all in, soaking up the collective power of awe and intention. 2,500 men and women in a Las Vegas hotel auditorium, simultaneously dreaming, expanding, imagining new futures, and magnetizing abundance. I feel like a million bucks.

Then Tony hones in on a muscled man, shining with good health and oxygenated skin. And yet, the man looks defeated. He cannot see how he could possibly raise his prices; he cannot imagine how he could go from being a gym owner to a million-dollar magnet. He is as buff as I am small. But we are both brick-and-mortar business owners. He has his fitness. I have my music. We are both skilled at what we do. I see myself in this man.

"How much do you charge?" asks Tony. The man tells him.

"How much do your competitors charge?" It's almost double.

This man, who has walked his walk and talked his talk and has the physique and cardiovascular health to prove it, is charging his clients below the market-related rate. He believes his clients will not value his services enough to pay more. I am charging below market-related rates. His beliefs are my beliefs. And Tony is exposing them for what they are: An argument for our limitations.

> **Gold Nugget**
> *How you perceive the value of your own product or service dictates how others perceive it. If you don't believe in your own value, how can you expect your clients to?*

Participant: "I'm afraid that if I raise my prices, my clients will leave, and I'll lose business. Plus, I worry they might think I'm only in it for the money."

Tony Robbins: "Charging what you're truly worth isn't about being greedy or money driven. It's about honoring the value you bring to your clients' lives. When you undervalue your services, you unintentionally create a perception that they are of lower quality or less valuable. By raising your prices, you demonstrate confidence in your abilities and attract clients who are serious about their fitness goals and willing to invest in themselves. It's important to focus on clients willing to invest in their own transformation. You're not just a personal fitness instructor but a transformational guide, helping people improve their lives. It's time to step into that role and charge accordingly. Your clients will benefit."

This man doesn't have a pricing problem; he has a self-worth problem. I don't have a pricing problem; I have failed to acknowledge my value. I am the bottleneck.

Something unexpected happens. Without warning or premonition, an old familiar heaviness descends upon me. I feel as if a cushion is pressed to my face. My chest tightens, my energy drains, and the chasm between me and everyone widens. I hear the words spoken, but I cannot take anything in. I want to fight the feeling. This can't be happening now. I try to avoid despair. I need air. I walk out of the room as fast as my crutches will carry me.

The nihilism that comes unannounced is the compound emotion of my upbringing: The abandonment, the isolation, and the unpredictable abuse. It's the real reason I'm here. I am the bottleneck. If I can't fix myself, I can't fix anything.

Gold Nugget

Prioritizing mental well-being isn't a luxury; it's paramount. No business strategy can overcome the barriers we place on ourselves if our thinking isn't right.

A man at the back of the auditorium opens the door for me, and I step outside into stillness. In the atrium, people wear orange T-shirts with clipboards, earphones, and mouthpieces. They are part of Tony's support team. My distress must be visible because one of them approaches me:

"Hey, how are you doing?" she asks.

"Okay," I answer, "just... I'm just trying to... I'm having a hard time concentrating at the moment."

"Do you need some help?" She asks.

"Sure," I say.

She leads me to a quiet, private corner.

"I don't want to miss what's going on in there," I say, looking towards the double doors of the auditorium as if I've stopped to tie my shoelaces on the last leg of an Olympic race.

"OK, no worries. This won't take long," she says kindly.

She tells me to think of a moment when I felt on top of the world. I go straight to the symphony: the orchestra behind me, people on their feet, knowing I've nailed it.

She prompts me to recreate the moment in detail, to engage all my senses. "What is your physicality? What are you thinking? How are you breathing? Can you stand like that now? Can you talk to yourself like that now?"

I follow her prompts, and the block dissolves.

"How do you feel now?" she asks.

"Totally fine," I say, surprised at the results of this 'quick' intervention. I go back into the auditorium.

Inside, Tony is stirring up the audience: "There can be no should, only must. The degree of your hunger determines the degree of the outcome."

I am nothing if not hungry.

I am very well acquainted with the word 'hungry.' In the months and years following my experience in Boise, one of my college friends had asked what changed in the beginning that led to so many experiences in my life with God. I replied, "Hunger. Before, I never hungered to know Him." It is a hunger that drives me. We must have it in every area we want to grow. Hunger and passion. The degree of your hunger will determine the degree of your success.

I leave Business Mastery with the same 'wild curiosity in the face of the unknown' that I had when I left the crusade in Boise. I am fired up and fueled by ambition. I want to fly with the eagles.

Over the next 18 months, I learn the discourse of online marketing: SEO, funnels, lead generation, inbound marketing, outbound marketing, brand strategy, Facebook ads, average cart values, OTOs, downsells, upsells, order bumps, and avatars. I learn how to build a better website. I learn about irresistible offers, closing, connecting, high tickets, low tickets, and everything-in-between tickets. I opt into one-year programs. I join online communities. I sign up for seminars, masterclasses, and workshops: The 90 Day Year with Todd Herman; Impacting Millions with Selena Soo; ASK Method Masterclass with Ryan Levesque; Social Media and Selling Online with Rachel Pederson; Funnel Hacking with Russell Brunson. I traverse the south and west of America, from Alabama to Tennessee, from California to Chicago, from Nevada to Florida.

Gold Nugget

In life and business, stagnation is decline.
Continuous learning and adaptation are a must
to not only survive but thrive.

To keep growing, I've got to keep going.

GEMS OF WISDOM FOR CHAMPIONS

Your journey starts when you recognize the power within. Business mastery isn't about conquering external worlds but understanding your internal one.

The pathway to success is paved with self-awareness. Recognize your value, know your worth, and the world will align with your vision.

Belief systems define your reality. Challenge them. Change them. And you'll change your world.

You are not a product of your circumstances, but a result of your decisions. Every choice creates a ripple. Take ownership and responsibility and never pass blame.

There's a vast difference between interest and commitment. When you're interested, you do it when it's convenient. When you're committed, you accept no excuses, only results.

Business, at its core, is about solving problems. The bigger the problem you solve, the bigger the reward (and income!). What problems are you passionate about solving?

Your hunger drives you. But it's your passion that will determine how far you go. Feed them both.

Turn your cannots into cans and your dreams into plans. The world doesn't need more dreamers; it needs doers.

Twenty-Seven

NAMING NIGHTMARES: A SIMPLE MISTAKE'S HIGH STAKES

"Just as every piece of music starts with a single note, every business begins with a singular vision. Keep refining until the vision is clear—clarity is key!"
—Patricia Bartell

Before Google, before Yahoo even, we had the Yellow Pages. The chunky, anachronistic printed directory occupied cupboard space close to a telephone in every American household. It had the most primitive ranking system; it started with A and ended at Z. So, to appear at the front of the index (or at the top of the rankings in SEO-speak), you wanted to call your business something starting with 'A.' My students always said: "I want to be able to play like you. I want to be able to play this piece or that piece..." Everyone wanted to 'be able to play.'

"It starts with A followed by B. Why not?" suggested Debby. It was decided. At Music City, I took the first step in building my own business: registering it as Able to Play. Rookie mistake.

Shortly after moving the school to our new, larger visible-from-the-street premises, I got a phone call from the local Chamber of Commerce. "Would you consider sponsoring a team?" the man asks. Then, before I can gather my thoughts, he adds, "By the way, what exactly *do* you do? Able to play Soccer, Able to play Basketball?" I have a branding problem. I changed the name to Able to Play Music. Next, I get a call from a curious parent: "I'm looking to buy a guitar. Are you a shop or a school?" I change the name to Able to Play Music Studio. This doesn't help. I get inquiries: Are you a recording studio or a school? Able to Play Music Academy just has no ring to it. Plus, it's not just me teaching anymore. I have several teachers working for me. And it's no longer just the accordion and piano. We're teaching all sorts of musical instruments. Clearly, we need a complete name change and a brand overhaul.

I draw my teachers, the parents, and the team into the name game. Nothing sticks. Eventually, one of my long-time students and dear friend, Marcia Lydisksen, calls me: "Patricia, I have the name. You won't like it, but this is what it has to be: Bartell Music Academy." I like the sound of it, and yet, it makes me uncomfortable. Putting my own name on the business feels like hubris, like mounting my own effigy on the wall. "Just put it to the team," Marcia urges. My staff's response is overwhelmingly affirmative. "This academy is your vision," they say. "People come because of Patricia Bartell, because of your reputation. You are the academy."

So, we have a new name. Now, we needed a new tagline. "What is our business, really? What do people want, really?" I have to clarify our purpose, passion, motives, and meaning. I recall Tony's intervention with Fitness Guy, and it comes to me in a flash: "Bartell Music Academy: Transforming lives through the Power of Music."

Gold Nugget

Your brand's name serves as more than an identifier; it's an embodiment of your story, ethos, and promise and becomes the first chapter of your business story. Each time you introduce your brand, it should echo the values you stand for and the transformation you offer.

I refine our elevator pitch: We don't just teach music; we teach life skills. We create leaders through music. We open doors for students to connect and develop a love for music. We produce rock stars of all ages.

I identify my unique selling point: We live in a microwave generation that values instant gratification, and I can get results fast. I can take an absolute beginner and get them playing in no time at all.

I learn 'to connect and understand at a deeper level' with The Bartell Academy's avatars: Students and, often, their parents. Our curriculum is tailored to each individual and how a person thinks and learns. If a child struggles to read in school, they will struggle to read music, but we have a unique way of teaching because we understand how the brain works. We work with the whole individual. We 'see' them and meet them where they're at, mentally and emotionally.

I innovate relentlessly. I am already in the mode of constant learning, always on the cutting edge of what's happening in pedagogy for piano and accordion, and always searching for ways to serve my students at a higher level. Before, I was curious; now, I'm compelled. I host globally recognized teachers and musicians like Fred Deschamps and multiple world champion winner Grayson Masefield in masterclasses with my students.

I plan ahead: August is our lowest income month. To keep momentum, I arrange mid-summer recitals and add summer camps and summer workshops to our offerings.

I also rebrand and relaunch our online music school, AccordionLifeAcademy.com, turning a brick-and-mortar business into a scalable entity. I add a bass course for beginners to the accordion curriculum by popular demand. I wish I had started with this course; it's what my target audience wanted most all along! What people need is often very different from what they want. I discovered this by watching YouTube videos and reading the comments and questions. I was active in Facebook groups where my audience would hang out, and again, there were dozens of comments and questions about how to play those little bass buttons. Once I learn to really listen to my audience and to respond to what they want, I shoot YouTube videos and begin posting regularly on social media, and the online school begins to grow.

I attend a conference on productivity run by Todd Herman, who works with elite athletes and entrepreneurs in the world of sports. He talks about the game, strategy, and the importance of practice. His language resonates deeply with me. Sport is much like music. To perform at our best when it matters most, we must first create a mental blueprint of the steps required to get there. We must visualize every move, every play, and every sound: hear it, see it, plan it, execute it.

I do this now: focus, visualize, and realize: I take a half hour every other day to hear the satisfying crunch of tires on gravel as parents park their cars in the lot. I hear their lively chatter as students come and go, their greetings, laughter, lightness, and love for the lessons. I hear the music filtering through the hallway. I see the kids in different bands rehearsing, performing, growing confident, and embracing their fellow band members. The academy is a nurturing container for our community. There are screens on the walls; our logo is mounted front and center. The music rooms are full, the teachers are busy, and our inbox is jam-packed with client inquiries. Lo and behold, everything I picture comes to pass.

Gold Nugget

Pricing isn't about what it costs you but about the value you deliver. As businesses evolve and grow, so should the perception of their worth in the eyes of their clientele.

Finally, nine months after Business Mastery, I raise my prices. None of my clients leave (except one who returns a few months later). This is a milestone, a breakthrough in my business, and in my evolution. As a result, the academy thrives.

GEMS OF WISDOM FOR CHAMPIONS

Growth is an iterative process. The first step may not always be right, but it leads you closer to where you need to be. The journey isn't a straight line from A to Z. Each step you take (action) will bring more clarity.

Every successful entrepreneur knows this: Understand your customer deeply. Their desires, their pains, their aspirations—they guide your business's course.

Our business is a direct reflection of the way we see ourselves. A powerful mindset is your strongest asset.

Value is subjective. It's not about what you think you're worth, but about what value you bring to your customers. When they see it, they'll invest in it.

Business isn't just about making money. It's about making a difference. So, as you scale the heights of success, always ask yourself, "Whose lives am I transforming?"

And remember—money will magnify who you really are on the inside. The more you make, the more it exposes you. Check your motives, intentions, and stay accountable.

Twenty-Eight

EMBRACING TRUTHS AND REDEFINING NARRATIVES

"When the engine is fine-tuned, it's the driver's mind that makes the difference."
—Patricia Bartell

"*B*usiness," says Tony Robbins, "is 20 percent mechanics." I've thrown myself into engineering my success with the hunger, muscle, and focus of a Formula One driver speeding around one corner after another. Define my cutting edge. Check. Clarify my message. Check. Rebrand. Check. Market. Check. Raise my prices. Check. I feel capable, efficient, and successful. If it could be learned, I had or would learn

275

it. I have sought out the kings and queens of each category, absorbed everything they had to teach, and predictably, my business speeds towards the six-figure bracket. But when it comes to the '80 percent psychology,' I feel as green as a first-time driver stalling in the slow lane.

I make notes eagerly. What are my strengths, weaknesses, traits, tendencies, preferences, and prejudices? Through teaching, I've learned about logical and creative thinkers and different learning styles but never looked under the hood of personality. Who is Patricia Bartell? What does she love, what does she value, and what does she choose to create?

I study a little Neuro-linguistic Programming (NLP), the connection between language, thought, and behavior patterns. I locate myself in the many models and variant quadrants of personality profiling. I reflect on the Six Human Needs: certainty, variety, significance, love/connection, growth, and contribution.

I am uncovering more of who Patricia Bartell really is

Gold Nugget

Deep introspection is the foundation for every successful entrepreneur. Knowing oneself, one's triggers, strengths, and weaknesses paves the path to sustainable success.

I have a new level of self-awareness and new tools with which to work. There is so much more to learn. I am living more intentionally and excited to be alive and in love with life. I want to be that same storm-tossed tree who left Boise with her roots digging down in search of life's great mysteries, her branches reaching skyward to touch possibility.

But I have no roots. I have grown up without knowing my biological parents. I have had no one to mirror me. I looked like nobody. I behaved like nobody. I could not be certain of my birth name, my birth date, or even my exact age. And because of early childhood trauma, I have no memory of life before the farm and very little of life on the farm. My branches want to reach upward, but I am psychologically starved of root food.

Underneath my enthusiasm, the uninvited darkness waves like a yellow flag on a sharp turn. I may be done with my past, but my past is far from done with me.

Gold Nugget

Hidden traumas and unresolved past experiences can be silent saboteurs of your business journey.
Every time you hit a financial ceiling, look for the limiting belief that is keeping you from advancing.

RE-VIEWING THE PAT

It starts as an isolated incident, in the witching hour, between sleep and wakefulness. It comes out of nowhere, this feeling that I am dying or disappearing or both. An intangible heaviness weighs me down, pressing against my chest. At the same time, I feel as if I'm slipping, slipping, slipping away. I reach for my nightstand, for the light, for something that feels real. I am grasping for consciousness, fighting to surface. But my mind is lagging, my body is not my own, and neither can lead me from this strange place between knowing and nightmare. The only thing I can do is pray, "Please, God help me wake up." The heaviness releases its hold on my chest, and I sit bolt upright, my heart racing. Although I have no sense of time, it's probably over in seconds.

These inexplicable attacks of brief terror happen randomly once every six months, then every other month, then every other week, then every other night, and eventually, I become afraid even to take afternoon naps, lest I get caught in the twilight of half-consciousness. It is no coincidence that these 'nocturnal visits' start just as I shift into a higher gear of self-mastery, honesty, and emotional intelligence. I recognize them as a desperate attempt by my outworn defenses to drag me back to sleep. But I choose to take them as a calling card: It is time to deal once and for all with the trauma of my childhood.

Someone once asked me, "Why now? Why do these nocturnal visits happen especially when you're seemingly at your happiest?" On my spiritual journey, two different people I hold in the highest regard told me the same thing at different times. "It is the body telling you that you are ready to deal with this trauma. It's probable someone early in your life, at the orphanage, tried to smother you with a pillow to take you out. These nocturnal events are happening now because now you have the tools and understanding to handle the truth."

I have read a comment on the Tony Robbins Facebook page about a retreat called the Hoffman Institute. "Tony is great, but man, these people go deep." I google 'Hoffman Institute.' Its tagline reads: "When you're serious about change." I sign up.

As I start to fill out the paperwork, I have reservations about what I'm getting myself into. The protocol is intimidating: No makeup. No jewelry. No mobile phones. No mention of what you do for a living, first names only. And only one emergency point of contact outside the walls of the retreat is allowed. We are expected to show up without armor and ready to 'do the work.'

Driving along the winding road that takes me through Napa Valley to the beautiful town of St. Helena and on to the retreat, I marvel at the rows of stately Redwood trees and pristine vineyards. The neat symmetry promises order and harmony as if the landscape itself has been 'Hoffmanized.'

Gold Nugget

Shedding pretenses and truly understanding oneself are the secret sauce of success. Authenticity is magnetic and draws people and opportunities.

Approaching the Institute's 45-acre leafy grounds, I think to myself, "How hard can this be?" At reception, I find a workbook journal with my name on it. "Welcome, Trisha," it says. I am immediately triggered. Nobody calls me Trisha. That's what my family called me on the farm. (Except for my older sister Phyllis, who called me Rennie "because you are like a little bird," she'd say.) Trisha is the name tag for an outworn identity. It's a dress I don't care to wear. Trying to hide the churning inside, I tell the smiling receptionist that there has been a mistake, "My name is Patricia," Trish for short, if she must. "This week, you'll be called Trisha," she responds sweetly but with an authority that leaves no room for negotiation. She says, "Everything is designed to trigger you, so together, we can support you and deal with this once and for all." And so, it begins.

For the next week, we are led through a process that combines neuro linguistic programming, cognitive behavioral therapy, bioenergetics, psychodynamics, journaling and reflection, mindfulness meditation, group discussions, and a lot of physically expressive work. There are many breakdowns and breakthroughs. "Lean into the pain, dig deep, forgive, let go," the facilitators urge.

Our days are scheduled from breakfast to dinner; even our sleep is monitored. At times, we are asked to eat in silence and to keep journaling after meals. It's our prescribed 'homework.' As a sociable person, I find silence hard. But I find emotional expression even harder. Despite all Debby's efforts over the last decade, my vocabulary for feelings is not much wider than that of a Spot the Dog Reader for first graders.

I have three default responses to the question: How are you? Fine, good, and great. Unsurprisingly, all three go-to words are banned on the retreat. Instead, I am given a piece of paper as an emotional reference. It lists 50 nuanced feelings from 'anxious' to 'vulnerable.' I feel like a tourist in Paris consulting a pocket phrasebook so that I can ask for directions to Notre Dame. Instead of pathways to a cathedral, I'm following synapses to my prefrontal cortex, that part of the brain that links words to emotion. And, as happens to tourists in Paris, I often get lost.

Trauma is not something that happens to us; it is something that happens within us. It is caused by a sense of perceived helplessness and unbearable pain. In times of emotional unease, it triggers a reflexive defense mechanism that constricts our ability to engage, to be fully present in the moment. It is the keloid to our psychic scars.

Children who suffer severe trauma are known to disconnect from their intuitive selves and thus from their authentic selves, too. They live to please, strive to impress, and crave acceptance and belonging. Because they have not been seen for who they are, they cannot value who they are. And therefore, they seek constant validation through what they do, how well they do it, and how much of it they do. I worked harder, practiced more, and pushed myself further because I needed recognition; I craved love.

The salient belief of the Process is the importance of childhood or, more precisely, the emotional discovery of the truth about the unique history of our childhood. We must become conscious of and disconnected from learned patterns of thought and behaviors.

Barbara was judgmental. So, I was judgmental. While Barbara judged others. I turned that judgment inwards. She was critical of me. I was critical of myself.

I believed that I was not wanted. I was not pretty enough. Not smart enough. Not loveable. I was always trying to prove myself. I was short. I fell short of my own expectations. I asked constantly, "What is wrong with me?"

These patterns spilled into adulthood like a water jug with holes in its sides. If a student left the school to immigrate with their parents, I'd ask myself, "Did I do something wrong?" or "Could I have done more for them?" Debby would say, "Students come and go." But I could not let go. If there were a situation with a colleague, a staff member, or a musician, I'd assume it was my fault. As a learned reflex, I'd always wonder, "Have I made a mistake?"

But the process does not abandon us to our past. Whatever or whoever the root cause of my broken self may have been, the result, here and now, is self-reliance, self-determination, and an extraordinarily high standard of excellence. I feel an inkling of gratitude, even for Barbara.

We are the stories we tell ourselves. I must tell a new story. During the week, we are asked to journal back to our origins to own our narrative. I had built an entire identity around being an orphan, on the belief that I was unwanted and the corollary, that there was something fundamentally wrong with me. Now I ask myself: What if this were a flawed premise, a hypothetical history? And in the absence of fact, was I not free to adopt a different, equally plausible narrative?

What if I were not born in prison, abandoned, or unwanted? What if my fifteen-year-old mother was not allowed by her conservative Catholic family to keep me? What if my father had to work to support me, and so handed me to his older sister to raise alongside her own children? What if I was handed over to the orphanage as an act of sacrifice because that was the only place where I could receive the medical treatment that I desperately needed? What if my illness was life-threatening and the need for treatment so urgent that my aunt did not have time to collect my parents' signatures? What if, in an attempt to cut through red tape, she had ticked them off as 'in prison?' That would have made her my guardian and signatory. I had survived against enormous odds. What if I was wanted and marked out for a higher purpose?

> ### Gold Nugget
>
> *Remember, you have the pen. If an old story doesn't serve you, write a new one that empowers your journey ahead.*

After the exercise, I feel peaceful, hopeful, and complete. And I say so without once looking at the emotional reference map.

On the final day of the process, we all reveal our last names and professions. Among us are celebrities, socialites, and captains of corporate America. It doesn't make a bit of a difference. To each other, we are simply fellow humans, emptied of hurt and full of forgiveness. Sometimes powerful, sometimes doubtful, we are brothers and sisters who have walked alongside one another for a few short days on a journey toward our most authentic selves.

I drive away from the Hoffman Institute with new awareness: I had no idea how broken I'd been, how thin the thread on which my life had hung. I had dared to look unblinkingly at the past. But I had no intention of getting stuck there. Tony Robbins says, "Identify your problems, but give your power and energy to solutions." I look straight ahead.

GEMS OF WISDOM FOR CHAMPIONS

Embrace every aspect of who you are – the light, the dark, the strengths, and the vulnerabilities. The degree of your own personal acceptance of yourself will be the degree the world (and your customers) accept you.

Your past can anchor you or propel you. The choice is yours. Every day is an opportunity to rewrite your story. The journey inwards is as significant as the journey outwards.

Remember, confronting your past is not about dwelling, but about understanding, healing, and using it as *fuel* for a brighter tomorrow. And speaking of a 'brighter tomorrow,' spend more time dreaming and creating the future you want so your past doesn't hold you back but serves as a launching pad!

Twenty-Nine

DEFINE YOUR WHAT, ANCHOR YOUR WHY

"Your 'what' is the journey you've traveled, your 'why'
is the purpose that journey gave you."
—*Patricia Bartell*

I've deep-dived into my past. I have spent uncountable hours and as many dollars exploring my psychological makeup. I have studied non-stop and acquired an arsenal of marketing and leadership skills, all in the name of saving my business. Now, the academy is growing exponentially, and AccordionLifeAcademy.com is all but running on autopilot. And I must revisit the 'what' and the 'why' that stokes my hunger.

The answer does not reveal itself at once. For a time, I roll on the momentum of progress and a thirst for growth. There is a truism in the entrepreneurial world: 'You don't know what your next step is until you take it.'

I continue to attend live events. Tony Robbins' Unleash the Power Within, Knowledge Business Broker, Date With Destiny, and Leadership Academy Training; Legacy Mastermind with Brian Delaney; Nail it and Scale it with Kerwin Rae. Ironically, the next piece of the puzzle falls into place *before* the doors even open to these events, while I wait in line.

I am almost always among the first attendees to arrive at an event. If the doors are scheduled to open at 8 a.m. sharp, I'm there by 6:30 a.m. I have a theory that you can quantify a participant's level of hunger by the time of their arrival. There is always a small pack hungry enough to be the first through the gates. Like the Apple watches, our early arrival marks us out as a sub-tribe: The Hungry Ones, the ones willing to go all in and do whatever it takes. We can spot each other, the wolves, with no plan B for our A game.

We make up an eclectic queue of early birds: chiropractors, inventors, pet-store owners, people in health and wellness, and education. The ice-breakers are always the same: "What business are you in?" "Why are you here?" and "What are you struggling with?" People tell me about their challenges, and I slip instinctively into problem-solving mode. I have been doing this with my students for years. When they struggle to play a piece of music, make the same mistake repeatedly, or cannot find their flow, my brain automatically goes into overdrive: "How do we deal with this? What do I need to give them to execute better?" I would read my students, I would see the problem, and I'd visualize the solution. I'm doing the same thing now. The teacher in me has simply switched hats from music to marketing.

Gold Nugget

Your skills in one domain can always be transferred to another. The core remains in understanding people and problems.

On their face, their challenges are either technical, relating to websites and Search Engine Optimization for example, or they're related to pricing structures. But scratch the surface, and the obstacles are almost always internal. It's an issue of perception and self-worth. There is a lady who sells dog food. Her product is premium, but she's following the Walmart model of low-priced leadership. She thinks she needs to undercut her competitors. I have witnessed enough interventions to know that I'm really dealing with flawed framing and faulty beliefs. Her product is excellent; the reviews are five-star. She is the bottleneck in her business. Her customers are not 'just' buying dog food; they are buying her story, her journey, her value, and all she's put into her business.

Gold Nugget

It's not just the product or service you offer. It's the stories, values, and emotions entwined with them that make the sale.

As I sit there, answering one person's questions, we're inevitably joined by a second person and then a third... "How would you do this? What do you think of that?" they fire at me. I start answering, and before I know it, there's a crowd gathered around me. "You're so good at taking complex ideas and making them simple," they say. And this is how I get my first clients to coach and my first podcast invitations.

Sometimes the questions are directed at my personal journey. For so long, I believed people saw me as 'handicapped' and therefore 'less than'. But in this context, my crutches are clearly seen as a symbol of resilience and overcoming. I speak as honestly as I know how about my own self-limiting beliefs, starting with the plaguing notion that something is wrong with me.

The conversations inevitably turn to money. Most of the attendees at these events have already achieved a degree of success. But they want to know what more they can do to break through the financial ceiling. "How did you do it?" they ask. I tell them the story of a ten-year-old girl running outside as her father pulls up to their farmhouse in a giant luxury motorhome hired for a rare family road trip. Young Patricia is awed by its size and grandeur, by its sleek lines and metallic curves. The motorhome is impressive by any standards but for a little girl raised on the smell of an oil rag, it's downright dazzling.

She asks excitedly, "How much did *that* cost?"

"Oh, you won't be able to handle it," her dad answers.

It's an off-the-cuff comment mostly likely blurted without agenda. But, it encodes itself like a superbug in her impressionable brain and grows like bad bacteria into a false belief about her capacity to manage large sums of money. "I can't handle it!" she thinks.

"I had to go all the way to the source to rewire my beliefs about abundance," I tell them.

Gold Nugget
The barriers in business are often mirrors, reflecting our internal limitations and biases.

People want to hear my story, and I have a message to share. In *Man's Search for Meaning*, Victor Frankl writes, "Success, like happiness, cannot be pursued; it must ensue. And it only does so as the unintended side effect of one's personal dedication to a cause greater than oneself or as the by-product of one's surrender to a person other than oneself." In these lines, waiting for the doors to open on workshops and events that promise to lead me to success, I find my What and my Why.

My 'What' is my story. And, my 'Why' is to give love, life, and light to others by sharing my life's lessons. I wonder: Is this what God intended when I received that message in the healing room all those moons before, "And I will give you the nations?"

There is a second part to my 'Why.' Music has been a gift to me, especially the accordion. I desperately needed the physicality that playing it required; the intense focus to coordinate the basses, the bellows, and the keyboard. But the accordion world is dying. I must do my part to revive it. My story is embedded in the accordion's story. If I can share my story with the world, perhaps I can generate new interest in this strangely beautiful and endangered instrument that has served me so well.

The next stage in my evolution starts to take shape: If I'm to gather an audience, I must build my personal brand.

Thirty

HARNESSING THE ADD BUSINESS BRAIN'S GIFT

"The beauty of our brains isn't in its perfection, but in its ability to evolve, adapt, and overcome."
—Patricia Bartell

Our beliefs inform our thoughts. Our thoughts inform our feelings. Our feelings inform our actions. This idea is as simple as it is revelatory. In practice, however, it requires vigilance. I start dissecting my beliefs and looking at my thoughts under the microscope of awareness. I become an emotional vivisector.

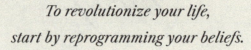

Gold Nugget

To revolutionize your life,
start by reprogramming your beliefs.

I had lived so much of my life unconsciously. Now I'm determined to challenge every notion that I've ever held. It becomes a game I play until there is not a single unexamined thought on the board.

I had just completed Wealth Mastery with Tony Robbins, and by now, I'm quite familiar with the concept of money beliefs, money roadblocks, and relationships with money. I've gone from barely being able to speak about money to loving the subject. Money is energy; selling is a gift you give to people. Now, sitting on the deck, reviewing Wealth Mastery and my relationship with money, a question pops into my mind: "Are there any other areas of my life with which I don't yet have a good relationship? The answer is instant. My mind. It's the last nagging question: "Is something wrong with my mind?"

I cannot remember being in the orphanage. I could not memorize dates in history class. I have almost no recollection of foster care, and I struggle to retrieve mundane memories of the farm. I wonder, did the nightmare experiences of my infancy and childhood irrevocably damage my brain?

And this is how I come to be positioned on a narrow gurney-type table with my head on a special headrest and instructions to lie as still as possible. It's the 17th of June, 2021. I'm at The Amen Clinic, Bellevue, Washington State. A sophisticated scanning machine rotates around my head. It's capturing gamma rays emitted by the radiotracer that's been injected into my arm and accumulated in the target organ: my cerebrum. The acquired data will be processed by a computer to create a three-dimensional image of my brain.

The wet flaps of the cortex, this vast wiring of nerves and synapses, sitting in an electrically charged soup of chemicals, hold the mysteries of my memory, musicality, personality, dark moods, and bright joys, loves, and dislikes. It is essentially *me*. For a brief moment, I feel like I'm trespassing into a forbidden, sacred space: The Secret Archives, the Ark of the Covenant, The Holy of Holies—my brain. "Too late to walk this back," I think to myself. My arms and legs are strapped to the bed.

The scan takes about 20 minutes. Before the scan, I was put in a little room with a desk and computer and instructed to 'click as fast as I can,' chasing random patterns of words, numbers, and pictures on a screen. The scan must capture an image of my brain in its 'active state.'

The next day, the scan is repeated. But this time, it's interpreting the functions of my brain in its resting state. I'm first led to a dark, soundless room where the blinds are drawn. No light, no noise, no phone. "Just relax," says the nurse. Half an hour later, she fetches me and walks me silently back to the gurney bed.

The generated images are analyzed by a specialist trained to identify any abnormalities or areas of concern.

I have concerns.

> **Gold Nugget**
> *Whether through trauma or trials, our brain has an incredible ability to adapt, heal, and grow. What you see as defects might be the hidden treasures waiting to be tapped into.*

I have been working with a personal life coach, Veenu Keller. I give her background on my childhood and my fascination with the brain, how we learn, and how we think. I mention that I struggle with memory. She tells me about a prominent psychiatrist and brain health expert: "The number one neuroscience guy on the planet." Dr. Daniel Amen has extensively studied neuroplasticity—the brain's reorganization ability by forming new neural connections and pathways. He is working with former pro football players, trying to help them recover from head trauma likely caused by hard hits on the field. But the brain can suffer from emotional trauma too. Prolonged, intense stress, especially in childhood, disrupts interactions between the amygdala, hippocampus, and prefrontal cortex, leading to difficulties recalling specific details or periods of time.

Mind you; she does not use these words. And neither do I. What she actually says is, "I have heard that trauma can cause holes in the brain, making it look pretty much like Swiss cheese."

"That's it!" I think. "That's what's wrong with me. I have Swiss cheese for a brain." Toxic beliefs are rarely rational.

Veenu tells me about Dr. Amen's program to become a licensed brain trainer. The program includes techniques and tools for teaching brain health optimization. I can integrate it into my coaching and teaching practices. My clients, students, team, and I will benefit from increased focus, creativity, and resilience. As an added incentive, Dr. Amen offers a discount on his program with special pricing for the neuroimaging scan. I know that at some point, one of my clients will ask me about the scan, and I never lead my clients where I have not already gone. It's a guiding principle that I've applied diligently to my music practice; it's what pushed me to compete in the World Championships. How could I have groomed future champions if I had not reached that level myself? It's this thinking which motivates me now. I take the program. I get my license. And here I am, waiting for the results of my scan.

We're still in the throws of the Covid pandemic, and the world is turning at a snail's pace. After three months, I eventually have a Zoom call with the specialist physician who conducted my study. I've been counting the days to this meeting, but now that it's time, I'm unsure if I want to get on the call. What am I going to see? Black spots of limitation? Shadows of sadness or instability? Gray areas of grief? Or worse, Swiss cheese?

The doctor explains what I'm looking at as he opens my files. "I'm going to show you the picture of the outside of your brain, and then we're going to look at the inside of your brain," he says. He points the cursor: "This one is your brain, and this is the demo brain."

My brain is beautiful! A magical kaleidoscope of cerulean, yellow, green, and red woven synapses. The contours of cognition, thought, knowledge, all the curves the mind preserves. It looks even better than the demo, brighter and more vibrant. "It's a very healthy brain," he says, smiling. "Now, let's look at the inside."

He changes the image. The top two images show my brain in its active state and the lower two in its resting state.

"What is interesting," he says, "is that in its resting state, your brain is still active." He has highlighted a vague diamond shape. He explains that the diamond pattern and the two slight indents he's circled in the prefrontal cortex are associated with past emotional trauma that has pushed the brain into overdrive. "Okay," I say, exhaling slowly. "Why, then, does my brain not look like Swiss cheese?"

"Two reasons," he says, "your music and your mindset."

Practicing, playing, or even listening to a musical instrument stimulates neuroplasticity and releases dopamine, a neurotransmitter linked to emotional regulation. Additionally, years of musical training have improved my memory, attention, and overall cognitive abilities. Similarly, a 'growth mindset' reduces negative stress on the brain and fosters emotional regulation and resilience. I had unintentionally been healing my brain for years. "The damage is so slight that it's almost undetectable," he reassures. I breathe a sigh of relief.

Then, a few days later, I get a follow-up phone call from a gal at the Amen clinic. She is suggesting various supplements. "This will help with your ADD," she says. "No," I say emphatically, "I don't have ADD."

"Well," she says, "it's in the notes."

"Well," I say," "there's been some sort of mistake. I spoke to the physician, and he never mentioned ADD. I have a whole music academy. I work with ADD kids. I do not have ADD." I end the call and immediately schedule another appointment with the physician.

That old nagging question, "What's wrong with me?" bounces back with the force of a basketball slammed against a wall by a seven-foot NBA player. Whack. It hits me in the head. I knew it. There is something wrong with my mind.

For all my denial, the label Attention Deficit Disorder, becomes a self-fulfilling prophecy. I go from doing things at the last minute to doing them at the last second. My days become chaotic. My stress levels go through the roof. I'm behaving like a rebellious child. I am annoyed with myself.

At last, the day of my appointment arrives. I get straight into it: "What's this about ADD?" I ask. The physician matches my hysteria with reassuring calm. "Patricia," he says, "you do have a very mild case of ADD, so mild that it has gone undetected until now. This is nothing to worry about.

"On the contrary, it's gotten you to where you are today. Why do you think you climbed the heights of music... and business? You have an entrepreneurial brain." He lists all the ways in which ADD acts as an internal driver: Creativity and out-of-the-box thinking, an ability to make unique connections and see possibilities that others might miss. Hyperfocus and intense passion. Higher tolerance for risk-taking. An ability to adapt to unexpected situations and the resilience to rebound from failure.

Gold Nugget

Your quirks, those things you see as faults? They might be the rocket fuel propelling you to unimaginable heights in business and life.

To mitigate the negative effects, he prescribes a planner to schedule my days and weeks and advises against multitasking. Perfect, I had already created my own planner, The Elite

Business Planner, which I use strategically to hit all eight pillars of business weekly:

Innovations, Marketing, Sales Process, Operations, Raving Fans, Financials, Personal Development, and Company Culture.

He also recommends changes in my diet, lots of protein, and added zinc, vitamin D, and iron. A severe iron deficiency would account for sudden dips in mood and energy.

The physician ends the call by saying, "Patricia, those indents in your brain are not limitations holding you back; they propel you forward. Your diamond brain has been a gift. You've used it. And so, I think its mission is accomplished. There is nothing wrong with you."

"There is nothing wrong with me." His words soothe like honey balm on burnt skin. My brain has been a gift. Just as my crutches have been a gift. The places where we've been broken are where the riches lie; the gold is in the cracks. "Keep your perfect offering," sang Leonard Cohen, "There is a crack, a crack in everything; that is how the light comes in."

I want to shout it from the rooftops: There is nothing wrong with me. I want to tell every person who has ever questioned themselves, who has ever felt 'less than' or damaged: There is nothing wrong with you.

> **Gold Nugget**
>
> *Our imperfections, our cracks, are not just the places where light gets in. They are the places from where our brilliance shines out.*

Limiting beliefs are the bars to your mental prison. Change your thinking, and those bars disappear, liberating the real you. Redefine and embrace your imperfections. Turn them into superpowers. There is a crack in everything. That is how the light comes in.

GEMS OF WISDOM FOR CHAMPIONS

Stop for a second and think: Why do you find it easier to champion someone else's vision rather than your own? YOU have the power, the spark. Own your narrative and steer your business towards greatness!

Those quirks, those 'imperfections' you keep pointing out? They're not barriers; they're your secret sauce! They make you UNIQUE. Turn them into your trademark, and let the world see your authentic self!

Your perceived weaknesses? They're just strengths waiting to be understood. Flip the script! Discover the power that's been there all along, and let it revolutionize your business approach!

The marketplace is not just a place; it's a grand stage. And on that stage, every brand has a unique song to sing. Don't be afraid to stand out; let the world hear your distinct melody. Embrace it, amplify it, and watch the world dance to your tune! Don't be the world's best kept secret. Get your content out there everywhere so people can find you!

And remember ... you are enough, in every shade, tone, and frequency of your being. Every time you think there's something "wrong" with you, there's a whole universe inside of you functioning in perfect harmony, propelling you forward.

Go and step into your power, own your journey, and let your business echo your deepest passions!

Thirty-One

LESSONS FROM THE KING OF CLOSING

"Success is never a solo act; it's built on the wisdom of mentors and the enthusiasm of our tribes."
—Patricia Bartell

In the digital landscape, social media has become a crowded battleground, a noisy marketplace of self-promotion. People clamoring for attention, validation, and the chance to turn their online presence into a profitable career. Everyone's vying to become the next big thing; everyone's reaching for overnight success and viral infamy. Everyone's peddling hope and its big sister, fortune. It's a virtual talent show of 'experts' showcasing their skills and creativity in hopes of attracting a significant audience. The competition is fierce; the saturation is staggering. And I have no idea how to cut through the clutter. But I do know one thing, I want to make a big impact. So, the search began for an influencer course that could help me stand out and set myself apart. When I encounter a program called 'High-Ticket Influencer' with Dan Lok, the green light starts flashing. I know this is *it*. I sign up and schedule my discovery call.

Gold Nugget

Amidst the digital chaos, it's YOUR genuine voice that will command attention. Algorithms change but genuine human connections? They're timeless.

The next day, I receive a WhatsApp message from Dan Lok's right-hand man, Desmond. "Hi Patricia, to help make tomorrow's call even more efficient, why don't you shoot me a short voice message about what you have done, why you are interested in the High Ticket Influencer Program (HTI), how you know Dan Lok, and what motivated you to fill in the application. That way, when we get on the call, I can help you even faster."

I write back, "Hi Desmond, I'm a professional musician, teacher, and international adjudicator. And as much as I love music, I had to get into the business arena to learn how to grow my business before it collapsed. So, for the last three to four years, I've been fully immersed in the world of business and digital marketing. I have gone through training from top industry leaders, including Tony Robbins, Kerwin Rae, and Russell Brunson, (I was in Russell's 2CCX program for about a year.) My business in the music industry has grown and now I'm being sought out as a business coach because of the results I can bring my clients.

I've combined the two industries (business and music) as the music industry desperately needs new business coaches. I'm interested in the High Ticket Influencer (program) as I was trained by the NBC producer of the Today Show on 'how to be on camera.' I've produced hundreds of videos for courses, and I'm now switching to grow my YouTube channel and want to build a premium offer. As a musician, I'm no stranger to the stage, but now I want to show up as a Power Speaker.

I'm looking to grow my brand, improve my video presence and be a strong, compelling influencer who can close any stage, whether on camera, webinar, or on an actual stage. I see that Dan Lok covers all of this in this particular program [High Ticket Influencer].

I came across Dan's videos on Facebook, watched several videos on YouTube, and I just got his course on "Unlock the Millionaire Within." I've already watched several videos in there, and I absolutely love it. I've been looking for training that will not just take me to the next level but will put me into the next field of play. This is why I filled out the form.

Hopefully, that info helps, and I look forward to speaking with you tomorrow. Have a great night."

The next day I'm face to face with Desmond over Zoom.

After a short dialogue, he suggests, "Well, why don't you join Dan's Five-Day S.M.A.R.T. Challenge? After that, if you like what he has to say, how he operates, and how he coaches, you can join the Influencer program."

I have done almost a dozen 5-Day Challenges during my business journey. Essentially, they are online coaching experiences where a mentor shares his or her expertise to help the audience achieve a specific goal or solve a problem. It usually takes place over five days (hence the name) though you might have a three-day or even a one-day challenge. And it usually takes place in a temporary "pop-up" Facebook Group.

Gold Nugget
In the entrepreneurial realm, stagnation equals death.
Continuous learning is a mandate for success. To stand tall,
you must wear the armor of relentless learning and swift
adaptation. And remember this ... the one who is in the game
longest wins. Don't give up on your dream.

For the coach or mentor, it provides time to establish trust and authority, prove their authenticity, and showcase their skill. During the challenge, prospective clients can decide if they resonate with the mentor's teaching style and whether or not what's on offer is a good fit for their needs. There is no hard sell; the mentor simply extends an invitation to work with them on a paid basis after the five days of the challenge are up. If the prospective client has found it useful, they're likely to opt in.

Gold Nugget

It's not about what it costs; it's about the massive transformation it triggers. Offer change, not just a product, and watch abundance flow to you.

The Challenge starts, and I quickly decided that I really like this guy. He is coming at things from a fresh angle, not offering a watered-down version of something I've already heard or dangling a golden carrot with promises of quick-fix algorithms.

"Let's build skill because if you build the right skill, you can take on any business and make it flourish," says Dan. He explains that marketing is only part of the equation. I need the skills of leadership, closing, digital marketing, and copywriting. I need a strategy so that my business can run itself sustainably and free me to grow. I need advanced mechanics to make my business unbreakable, to make myself unshakeable.

Dan himself started out as a copywriter and now has a reputation as 'the King of Closing.' A closer is someone who swoops in at the later stages of the sales process to turn leads or prospects into paying customers. Closers do what it says on the label; they seal the deal. To do so well, they must be skilled at building rapport, have deep insight into their customers' pain points, needs, and have superb listening skills. Watching Dan, I know I can learn from this man.

I throw myself into his S.M.A.R.T. challenge with all I've got. I'm the first to put my hand up as a volunteer, I wave to indicate understanding and enthusiasm, I give thumbs up in agreement, and I remain active in the group chat. I get Dan's attention. "Who's that woman?" he asks Desmond after the second day of the challenge. He wants to see my application form. Desmond tells him my vision, and Dan smiles. He gets it. He knows that I'm mentally prepared, that I've broken through the glass ceiling of my own limitations. I'm halfway there. "Get her on a call," he says, "I think we can help her."

Desmond sends me another note: "By the way, Dan noticed your participation; well done. He asked me about your model, and I explained your vision to him. He is keen to help..."

I never join the 'High-Ticket Influencer' program. Instead, I am invited to join Dan's Dragon100 group, an elite mastermind of six and seven-figure visionary entrepreneurs looking to scale their businesses sustainably. I asked for a hand; I got the whole arm! It takes over one year to work through Dan's prolific library of content and become the person I need to be to create the right team structures and business model. My academy now runs without me, freeing me to work on building my personal brand.

On November 11th, Dan sends me a message: "Do you want to do a Dragon Talk in December on Running Challenges?" The idea is to provide enough value in those 10 minutes that any of the Dragons might take it, implement it, and make six figures from it. "And here's your topic," says Dan: 'My Five Day Cash Machine: How to Successfully Package and Execute a Five-day Challenge'. I've watched the experts, and I've created frameworks for my own clients. This is my high ticket home. I've got this!

The talk is a resounding success. I am as comfortable speaking as I am playing the accordion before a live audience. And the Dragons respond accordingly. Afterward, Dan sends me another message: "Great job on the Dragon talk! Very well done. We should really get you to do more virtual events for your business. This is a strong skill we should leverage. Speaking at other people's events as well as your own."

The idea of 'closing from the stage' is not a new one. It's a slow-germinating seed that was first planted shortly after I attended Business Mastery in 2017.

Gold Nugget

You're not just a business owner; you're a story, a legacy.
Share it. Build your brand. Change lives.
Embrace the power of YOUR narrative.

At Todd Herman's '90 Day Year' conference on productivity, the lineup of speakers included a famous former athlete, all muscle, grit, and focus, even after his retirement. And when he talked, he didn't hold his punches: "Brought up in a broken family, my early life was filled with violence, poverty, and trouble. I became a ward of the State of California at the age of 12 and a prison inmate at 18. By the age of 22, my name was known worldwide as a champion." I listened with intent. The man was a four-time defending, undefeated mixed martial arts UFC champion. His name was Frank Shamrock.

Once Frank left the stage, I exited the auditorium for a bathroom break. I found him in the lobby, sitting alone on a couch. Usually, guest speakers of his stature would be whisked out the back door, but there he was, quietly minding his own business. I went to him to tell him how much his talk resonated with me. He invited me to sit beside him. What a picture we must have painted: The brawny retired fighter and the diminutive musician with her crutches resting against the couch. "Tell me a little bit about yourself," he said. I do. And when I finish, he asks, "Why are you not on that stage? You need to be on that stage." I tell him that my family is still around and that I have not yet found a way to frame the story of my upbringing that would serve a purpose without painting me as a victim. The only way I could tell my story and risk raising their ire was if it would have a transformative effect on other people's lives.

"My mama is still alive. She's sat in the audience, and she's heard my talk. She still thinks what she did was okay. It's your story. You don't need anyone's permission to tell it," he says. And with that, the tractor in my mind, churns the soil of suggestion. I had spent a large part of my life on stages. And all music is language. But it had not occurred to me until that moment that I might speak from the stage or that my voice might be my instrument.

And now, here is Dan Lok, saying out loud what I haven't previously found the courage to announce: I want to tell my story before live audiences; I want to 'close' from the stage.

In December 2021, I get another step closer to the dream. I'm one of five members of Dan's mastermind network shortlisted for the title, 'Dragon of the Year.' I'm standing at the front desk of the academy when I get the message. My phone pings. I look down, read it, look up, and tell my staff what it says.

The nomination is based on the Five I's. Integrity, Implementation, Improvement, Impact, and Involvement. Did you do what you said you were going to do? How quickly and how well did you implement what you learned from Dragon 100? How much have you improved your personal and business life since Dragon 100? How did you impact the lives and businesses of other Dragon 100 members? And how consistently did you engage in Dragon 100?

This is a big deal. My team goes wild. "You've got this, Patricia," they say, dancing around the room.

"It's only the nomination," I laugh.

"We don't care," they say, "in our eyes, you've already won."

Their joy is contagious, but if I want to win for real, there's work to be done. The finalists will compete at a three-day live event, 'Closers in Black.' Apart from intensives covering new strategies on closing, positioning, and leadership, vital skills to command six and seven-figure incomes, the event includes an award ceremony recognizing those who have excelled in various categories, and the Grand prize announcement: Dragon of the Year.

First, I must create a ten-minute video in which I *sell myself* and why I deserve to be Dragon of the Year.

Later in the day, left alone, the full weight of expectation sinks in, and the implications of the challenge settle in my stomach like a boulder on the seafloor. I have to sell myself. This is not Patricia talking about five-day challenges or giving instruction on a musical instrument. This is Patricia talking about Patricia. This is Patricia having to show up as herself, without an accordion to hide behind, convincing an audience of more than 800 attendees, many of them formidable businessmen and women, at a coveted live event to cast their ballot with her.

Once upon a time, I borrowed belief from Kendall. Now I borrow it from my team. I shake off self-doubt, roll up my sleeves, and get strategic. I research the challenge as If I'm auditioning for Shark Tank. I know what Dan wants: to promote his Dragon 100 program. I know what the voters want: to make more money. I know what the online audience wants: to hear how I went from cash flow problems to a thriving six-figure income. And I know what I want: to win.

My competitors all have strong stories. They are all powerful businessmen in their own right. They are worthy adversaries. But I have one strong advantage: I understand the art of performance. I know how to be persuasive on camera. Musical performance and speaking presentation have a shared DNA. Both aim to captivate the audience. Both demand practice to polish delivery. As musicians, we use dynamics, tempo, and phrasing to express a range of emotions; as speakers, we use vocal variation, gestures, and storytelling. Both take their listener on a journey. Both have a message. In creating magical moments for the audience, there is a harmonious convergence of melody and oratory. I am prepared. This is where I can shine.

Still, we have been given strict rules for the video: no fancy edits, no gimmicks, just us engaging our audience. And within the structure of our presentation, I know that I must include my story. This is the first time I'll be going public with my history. At home, late at night, I sit on the floor, leaning against the couch, pen and notebook in hand. I write. I erase. I write. I erase. I start again. It's harder than I thought. I want to inspire and motivate my audience. I want them to know that we are all alchemists and that beneath our base metals lies gold. I want them to know that their metaphorical crutches are not weaknesses but magical sticks that will take them where they need to go. There is a fine line between evoking pity or inspiration. I want to leave them believing that if I can do it, so can they. And that I can show them how. I put it all on the line.

Although the presentation is recorded, I do it as if it were a live event. I start with a question. "Investors, how many of you are here to have a six-figure day? Tell me 'YES' in the chat." And then I just go for it...

The day the presentation airs, I have Covid. I'm at the tail-end of a three-week bout of what feels like horrible flu. I'm on the couch with Debby and my King Charles Cavalier, Isabella. It's not the presentation I want to rewatch; it's the audience engagement, how they respond to me. My video is third in the lineup. Video one starts. The story is great. People are commenting. The second video plays—same thing. I'm number three. I brace myself. I hear my voice as if it belongs to a stranger: "Hello, Investors..." and the chat blows up. I can barely read the comments; they're scrolling so fast and furious. "It's working!" I shout through my nasal congestion. "It's working!" Debby's laughing. Isabelle's barking. I am beaming. The video ends with me giving a presidential wave goodbye:

"And thank you for voting for me," I say.

The winner is announced that afternoon. "The Dragon of the Year goes to ... Patricia Bartell." I get a message from Dan: "Patricia," he says, "you have a gift for this." It's as if the slow germinating seed has burst fully formed from the ground in time-lapse. I feel the branches reaching upward.

GEMS OF WISDOM FOR CHAMPIONS

The path to greatness isn't determined by where you start, but by the steps you take each day towards your vision powered by your 'why.'

Every challenge, every stumble, every 'no' – they're not setbacks. They're setups for your next big leap. Look for the gift in them then use the setups as launchpads.

What if the only barrier between you and your wildest dreams is the story you keep telling yourself? Nothing in your life will change until you change.

Ask yourself: What would you do if you weren't afraid? And if you couldn't fail, what would you do? Now, take that step. Leap into the unknown, and don't look back.

Business isn't just about profits and losses. It's about impact. It's about legacy. What mark do you want to leave on the world? If you chase and strive after money, you've lost. Just build and serve, and money is a byproduct.

Remember, my Champion, you are not just a participant in the game of life and business. You're a trailblazer, an influencer, a force to be reckoned with.

Your journey, your story, and your influence are just beginning.

Thirty-Two

THE ESSENTIAL STEPS OVERLOOKED BY MANY

"In the orchestra of life, let confidence be your conductor and faith your foundation."
—Patricia Bartell

I have very little time to bask in the after-glow of my victory. Just one hour after the 'Dragon of the Year' announcement, I'll lead a two-hour talk, "The Confidence Killers to Your Six Figures."

The talk forms part of the 'Closers in Black' event. Its official name is 'The Dragon Round Table.' Ten Dragons have been chosen to enrich the audience with their knowledge and perspective of business. Participants can move freely between dragon Zoom rooms, and the challenge is to hold their attention, hopefully for the full two hours. As the newly crowned Dragon of the Year, I know all eyes will be on me; except, energy-wise, I feel more wilted than Wonder Woman, and my voice is still recovering from Covid. I have two friends and a fellow Dragon on stand-by should my stamina falter. But as the session progresses, much to everyone's amazement, my own included, I get stronger and stronger. Such is the power of passion. I'm in my zone.

"PATRICIA, WHERE DO YOU GET YOUR CONFIDENCE?"

That's the question I'm most often asked. From my history - orphaned, crippled, rejected, and neglected - it might seem that confidence would be a foreign concept. But remember, every child is born with natural confidence, ready to conquer the world. Over time, through challenges and setbacks, we often lose touch with this innate self-assuredness. But with faith, choice, discovery, and determination, I found my way back to that inherent confidence. My belief is this: confidence isn't just built from external accomplishments; it's first a process of reawakening what's always been inside. With the foundation of this rediscovered confidence, I then fortify it with skills, experiences, and emotional mastery. This is why during challenging times, I always remind myself, "I was made for this."

IT STARTS AND ENDS WITH YOU.

We are all surrounded by a never-ending buzz of voices. They are the lights that shine through our drawn curtains at night, the billboards of uninvited opinion, the alarming flashlights of critiques, and the cautionary red lights of other people's judgments. But true confidence isn't shaken by external stimuli. It's an internal compass, guiding us through the stormiest of times.

As a professional musician, I had to learn this lesson the hard way, in the middle of concerts and music studios. The critics and the doubters were like off-key notes, trying to mess up the melody of my dreams. My past was full of struggles, disabilities, critics, and setbacks. Instead of questioning why this happened to me, I asked, "What is the gift in this?" "What can I learn from this?"

DO NOT 'PLAY' FOR THE APPLAUSE

I eventually learned that confidence isn't about impressing the crowd, proving them wrong, or getting them to like you.

It's about rediscovering who you really are inside, the one as a child who danced without a care. The one who knew their *worth*.

Initially, when I performed, I did it for others' acceptance. I learned that if I performed well, I was liked. If I didn't perform well, there were consequences. But it's not about acknowledgment, it's about *who* I became. It started with God's acceptance and love and then self-acceptance and self-love. I no longer play for applause; I do it for myself. Winning isn't about getting trophies or positive reviews but showing myself that I can rise above my challenges and make my melody heard.

CHOOSE CAREFULLY WHOSE VOICE YOU ALLOW IN

Finding this kind of confidence took work. The world can be a tough critic, quick to judge, and slow to understand. I learned to filter out the voices that didn't resonate with my truth. Most importantly, I learned to silence my inner critic. We are often our own harshest judge. It's time to be our own best friend. Think of your mind as a powerful computer. Every thought, belief, and opinion forms this impressive machine's software. Negative voices are like viruses that corrupt the system.

It's not that other people's advice, wisdom, and opinions are not valuable. It's about being highly selective as to whose voices we let in. My mentor, Dan Lok, had already been where I was going and left footprints to follow on the path to success and back to my inherent confidence. His words lifted me and led me to believe in my abilities. He provided crucial software updates.

UPDATE YOUR SOFTWARE

Rediscovering confidence sometimes means rewriting our story, focusing on our strengths, and embracing every part of our journey. I chose to rewrite my story and change how I saw myself. I had to find the gift in the painful parts of my past—from being given away by my birth mom to being rejected by my adoptive mom when I was five.

It's about taking control, not to build a façade, but to reconnect with our true selves. I became the composer of my life, not just a performer trying to please an audience.

CONFIDENCE IS FOUNDED IN FAITH

Still, it didn't matter how much I rediscovered my confidence, if It didn't have a firm foundation, it would fall. People would eventually let me down. I would let myself down. Only one would never let me down: the God I served. I recognized that without Him, I was incomplete. I am part of a divine design, with a unique role in this vast universe that only I could fulfil.

It dawned on me that God doesn't call the qualified. Instead, He takes the ones He calls, regardless of their circumstances or shortcomings, and equips them with what they need. He qualifies those called.

Every score I play is a reaffirmation of who I serve, my belief in myself, a celebration of my dreams, and a reflection of my joy in living my passion.

GET LASER FOCUSED

True confidence is about recognizing our inherent potential and aligning our actions with our vision. With each self-affirmation, we peel back the layers, moving closer to our authentic selves. It's about being laser-focused on your goals and having rock-solid knowledge (not just a belief) that you can achieve them. This clear vision and strong internal drive will steer your business to success.

Building upon that natural confidence from within is all about adjusting our beliefs, reshaping our emotional rules, and directing our feelings. It's about orchestrating a symphony of success from the notes that have always existed within us.

Several months after 'Closers in Black,' I say to Dan, "I'm stuck ... I have put all my efforts into scaling my business and working on my personal brand. I had an influencer reach out and tell me I'm too broad in my social media posts. They said I should strictly share business posts and not posts about my life. But in my heart of hearts, I want to be the Influencer Keynote Speaker Closing from the Stage. I was made for the stage, and personal development is my forte. I feel lost and a bit paralyzed today about what to do and where to put my focus. So, I'm reaching out."

He answers, "It's very easy to solve. Here's the exact plan; follow this to a tee, and you'll make your millions." In bullet points, he lays out a precise plan of action, from becoming an inspirational speaker like Nic Vujicic to the business aspect, 'Persuasion on Camera and on Stage.'

It's so simple and brilliant! I'm beyond grateful for Dan. I know what to do now. I have a blueprint.

GEMS OF WISDOM FOR CHAMPIONS

Every time you've felt inadequate, it was merely an illusion cast by society's limiting beliefs. Break free and witness the true power of your being.

You came into this world radiant with confidence and destined for success. Don't let the world dim that light; instead, shine brighter.

It's not about learning new ways but unlearning the chains of belief that have limited you. Liberate yourself from those shackles with the truth of who you *really* are and watch your natural confidence soar.

Your transformation isn't a long journey ahead; it's a quick return to the essence of your true self. Accelerate towards your destiny.

The legends among us, the 1%, have mastered the art of shedding society's limitations. Adopt their mindset and watch how your world changes.

Get Access to The 'Crush It' Communication Course Series

at PatriciaBartell.com/Bonus

Thirty-Three

CHANGE WHAT YOU SEE, AND WHAT YOU SEE CHANGES

"As we shift the lens of self-perception, the world's perspective shifts in response."
—Patricia Bartell

What we wear is of no trivial concern. It influences our confidence and the way we navigate the world. Plus, we're biologically wired to make assumptions based on appearance. I know this firsthand. On meeting me, strangers always do a full-length vertical scan. In my head, I assume they are making their own judgments about my physical stature. Later I would learn that how I see myself is how people see me. As I've grown in self-acceptance and self-love, the question from people has changed from, "What's wrong with you?" to "Who are you?"

I have never shied away from the spotlight, and at the same time, I have wanted to be invisible. In this regard, my accordion has acted as a loyal bouncer or protective big brother. I play it seated on stage, and its bulk provides a shield from prying eyes. Seen and unseen.

I have always been marked as different. At home, I was one of the dark-eyed, dark-skinned, dark-haired 'bad Indians' in otherness to the good Caucasian cowboys. At school, I was the girl without a date for the dance. At university, I hid behind baggy clothes and weight gain, advising my male friends who dreamed of asking out long-legged Norse goddesses. "Look straight ahead, and you'll miss her" was once relayed to me by a third-party bystander. I flicked the comment off like a nuisance mosquito, but the sting never disappeared. I wore a mask of exuberance; beneath it, the wounds of rejection ran deeper than the small indents in my diamond brain.

In truth, if someone had said, 'Wow, you look beautiful,' I probably wouldn't have heard it. In the more hidden corners of campus, I was too busy worrying about whether they would like me, whether they would accept me.

Growing up, fashion was seen as unnecessary, superfluous, at best a distraction, and at worst evil, just as drawing attention to myself was considered ungodly. I, too, saw fashion as a vanity, not because I'd bought into that ideology but because it seemed a better option than the *fait accompli* of my crutches. But I have gone deep, I've gone wide, I've tunneled all the way to the recesses of my brain, and it's time to address the elephant in the room, my appearance.

I have made great strides since Debby became my mom. I was twenty-five at the time but looked to be of indeterminate age. (Anywhere between my actual age and the far side of forty.) I wore my old soul on my sleeve. Debby bought me new clothes, shopped, and taught me to make choices. My new hair stylists (to the approval of The NBC producer) had me lop off my permed hair. At all the events I attended, I took notes on tailoring, the handbags, the shoes, and the jewelry, and I'd started to look better suited to the business owner I'd become. As I shed the internal baggage, my physical appearance changed. And people noticed. At a baby shower, two Russian ladies I'd bump into occasionally leaned across the table and said, "Ve're yust discussing zat every single year zat vee see you, you look yunger. How do you do zis?"

Change what you see, and what you see changes. Change how you feel and what others see changes.

All the self-development work I've been doing has led me to a new belief system. When I walk into a room now, I assume people will be drawn to my energy, not my height. I do not assume that my crutches are shorthand for 'handicap;' I see them as a symbol of resilience. They tell a profound story without me saying a word. They are an asset to be leveraged, not a shame to be buried. I want my image to reflect this new-found confidence. Finally, I've created the woman I am and am ready to recreate the image I project.

Gold Nugget

Genuine self-confidence isn't just an inner feeling; it becomes an outward magnet drawing people towards your purpose.

Despite my progress, I want the physical manifestations of my transformation to be more intentional. I want to strategically create an online and offline image that will actively announce me as an authority in my field and as an influencer. It's not for nothing we call it "Power Dressing." Appearance is one of the strongest communication tools we have. I intend to project an image that supports my brand: energetic but focused, premium but accessible.

I've been through dozens of short branding courses to lock down a logo. I've explored my Jungian archetypes - The Queen, the Magician, and their correlating colors - gold and black. I've determined my font (*Open Sans and Libre Baskerville*) and shapes: angular and geometric (verses soft and flowing). As my symbol, I've chosen the golden eagles I watched soar down from the Rockies, exiled to my bedroom on the Montana farm. They reminded me, then and now, of freedom, precision, and binocular vision. I have found my vision and my freedom. And I want my clients to find theirs.

Whether it's my logo or my 'look,' what I'm doing, in reality, is controlling the non-verbal narrative. Regarding my appearance, I want to say what I mean.

Gold Nugget

In business, controlling the non-verbal narrative is as critical as perfecting the elevator pitch.

The camera doesn't lie, but it does wash things out— your gestures, your features—while exaggerating your flaws—the dark rings under your eyes, the open pores around your nose, the faint glow of perspiration on your forehead. To master my on-camera makeup, I take online courses and become a regular customer with a lovely young lady, Bree, who works at a high-end cosmetic counter. Bree loves her job: "This is a good color for you ... Try this eyeshadow ... Lipstick or lipgloss?" she asks. I go along with it, willingly enacting a never-happened part of my lost youth, a little girl playing dress up.

Sometimes, investing in yourself doesn't translate immediately into dollars or clients, but it translates into self-worth that eventually becomes priceless.

One day, inspired by Bree, I go to Nordstrom to buy 'apply at home' eyelash extensions. I read the instructions carefully and try to apply them. I try for two days, but I just can't get the hang of it. I go back to Nordstrom. "I cannot figure these out," I tell the shop assistant. "There seems to be a production flaw; they just don't work." The lady at the counter looks at them, then looks at me as if I'm Crocodile Dundee, newly arrived in the big city after wrestling reptiles in the Australian outback. Although younger than me, she addresses me as 'honey.' "Honey," she says, "That there's the left eyelash that you've been tryin' to stick on your right eye." Clearly, I need more help than Bree can offer.

I decide to hire a professional image coach. Parmita Katkar is a former Miss India model and actress, and it's hard not to be intimidated by her beauty. But she has humor, playfulness, and confidence that is rare in an industry that I've come to understand can take itself all too seriously.

At our first meeting, she says, "Well, you've obviously done a lot of work on the inside. Now we need to have it reflect on the outside so you can attract the right clients to your work."

I start to understand what clothes make me look and feel good, how to dress for my skin tone, my body shape, and my extroverted personality. I learn to leverage makeup, on and off camera. The fact that applying bronzer in just the right place defines my cheekbones or that the right-shaped brow totally reframes my face is as game-changing as the advent of automated invoicing. Of course, it's not fashion or makeup I'm learning to appreciate, it's me.

The result is a transformative journey that has nothing to do with wearing expensive clothes or looking chic. It's about self-acceptance and stepping into my power. I have the right to take up space, to be seen, to dazzle, and to enjoy it.

To conclude our work together, Parmita has invited me to Chicago for a photoshoot. The end product is wrapping around a gift to myself.

24-HOURS BEFORE A SIX-FIGURE DAY

In Chicago, the wind of a studio fan blows through my hair. Parmita adjusts the light; then she adjusts the lens. She directs me into position. "Put your right foot forward, lean your left crutch back, then turn your head slightly, lift your chin a little, just a bit." I turn my face to the warmth of the lights. Parmita moves in for a close-up. She says, "You are beautiful," and I believe her. I feel six feet tall. When I see the images, I like the woman smiling back at me. I understand what this journey has been about: Love. All love. The little girl on the 9th step gets up to look at the photographs, too. She approves. Who I was. Who I am. Who I have still to become; whoever that is, she will be beautiful.

GEMS OF WISDOM FOR CHAMPIONS

Life isn't about finding yourself; it's about creating yourself. What image are you crafting today?

Your image isn't vanity. It's a visual testimony of your journey, resilience, and spirit. Own it, celebrate it, and let it shine.

How many times have you let the external world dictate your internal worth?

Each time you step into a room, ask yourself: Am I here merely to blend in, or am I here to lead and inspire? Am I here wondering if people will like me or am I here knowing they will like me, love me, and some will pay me a lot of money! (This is my belief every time I step into a room. If you're going to make up stories in your head, make up good ones!)

Remember, as a business owner or entrepreneur, you're not just selling a product or service, you're selling a vision, an experience, and, most importantly, yourself.

Thirty-Four

THE ULTIMATE CLOSING TECHNIQUE REVEALED

"Entrepreneurship isn't just about building wealth; it's about challenging norms, reshaping paradigms, and influencing futures."
—Patricia Bartell

*S*teve Jobs was considered the business world's best storyteller. He intuitively understood the effect of a compelling narrative: "The most powerful person in the world is the storyteller. The storyteller sets the vision, values, and agenda of an entire generation," he said.

Myron Golden is a God-given natural-born storyteller. He inspires his audience to be the best version of themselves. He does so by making them believe in their own heroic potential.

The first time I see him live in action on stage is at Russell Brunson's conference on lead generation and funnel hacking. His performance floors me. His signature story, which he tells in more detail in his book, *From Trash Man to Cash Man*, is framed by his knowledge of the Bible. In fact, his entire business framework is based step by step on the teachings of King Solomon.

Like me, Myron is a polio survivor; he wears a brace on one leg. He is a believer. He is a high-ticket mentor who has trained thousands of entrepreneurs to 'close' from the stage. I feel a strong affinity with this man.

I would have liked to sign up for his one-year mastermind there and then, but I could not afford it at that time. Three years later, I opt-in to his five-day challenge: 'Make More Offers,' I upgraded to VIP status, allowing me to watch him coach participants.

"It's not what you do; it's how you make them feel that wins over an audience," he says. Myron demonstrates how he preempts and clears away objections, how he clears the pathways and moves his audience from inertia to momentum. He is a master at the art of persuasion. He doesn't sell; he simply offers people what they ask for.

Gold Nugget

Real persuasion doesn't feel like selling;
it feels like fulfilling a deeply seated need.

When questioned about the high-ticket of his coaching program, Myron recites Genesis Chapter 3: "Lack cannot exist in your experience unless it first exists in your expectation." He explains: "I never make dead-end statements like 'I can't afford it.' That would allow me to take a nap on the couch of disempowering ideas; that would let me off the hook. I ask instead '*How* can I afford it?'"

I have had some success showing my clients how to package their skills as a high-ticket offer. But I realize that I can do better. I've missed a key ingredient: Instead of selling, I should be allowing. Instead of convincing people to do what they already want, I should guide them to get out of their own way. Before Myron's Five-Day challenge ends, I ask, "*How* can I afford it?" I pull three loans to join his program. He's been 'closing' me all along.

One day, I was inside someone's virtual live event, and the next, I'm inside their high-ticket program. I'm surprised at myself; at how easily I've been sold into both Dan and Myron's high-ticket programs without once experiencing that high-pressured sales feeling one often gets before making a nervous, expensive purchase. And the lightbulb goes on: I am happy as a lark to be inside these elite VIP programs. I'm paying lots of money, yet they were easy to say 'yes' to.

Once the penny drops, once I understand the number one tool needed to make more sales and be effective at making people feel good about buying from me, I can create a predictable cash flow. Now it's game on. Now I am infused with energy and excitement. Now I can start scaling the business I dreamed of.

It feels as if I spend most of 2021 on an airplane. Over the space of six months, Myron holds four or five intensive two-day events in Tampa, Florida. The events include Stage to Millions, Mouth to Millions, and Offer Master Live. It's a long haul from Spokane to Tampa, from the top corner of Washington State to the bottom point of America. "Is it worth it?" Debby asks. "Yes, I answer; this man is a fire hose."

It's not just Myron's energy, business strategies, and wisdom I wish to marinate in. There's his team and the high-profile entrepreneurs that attend his live events. As always, I arrive early, early enough to catch the sun rising over the Clearwater beachfront, where the sea glistens diamond-like and even the birds look wealthy. I watch as one high-level car after another pulls up, and one high-profile entrepreneur after another gets out. Myron arrives in his beautiful blue Rolls Royce and hands his keys to the valets. It's not the riches that impress me; it's the success. I have the same thought I first had when I arrived at Fred Deschamps' farm to train with world champions like Grayson Masefield.

"I'm swimming with the big fish now." These mastermind groups are as much about the connections made as they are about the knowledge received. My Facebook friend group is full of millionaires whose advice is only one DM away. I learned that money is a currency, an energy exchange, a game. When you start talking in seven and eight-figure days, the meaning of money changes. It becomes less about affluence and more about influence.

There are between forty and fifty of us in the group. We all dine together on the first night in Tampa. When I'm about to leave, I thank Myron for a wonderful evening. He hugs me and says, "I'm so glad you're here. I can't wait to see what you do."

One of the first things in my planner is to launch my six-figure day and my mastermind group.

I also enroll in a course on 'How to be a better Storyteller.' In business, people want to know what you do, but it's *why* you do it that really sells them. And for that, you need a good story.

Gold Nugget
A great product without a story is like a book without a title; compelling but overlooked.

There are hundreds of magnificent storytelling coaches advertised online. I opt into several different courses to check each one out, but I settle on Bo Eason, a former professional American football player turned playwright and storyteller. His storytelling journey began after his successful career in the NFL ended. He emphasizes the importance of physicality, vulnerability, and connecting with the audience on an emotional level. The promise of the program is that by its end, I will have crafted my three-minute signature story.

I work closely with one of Bo's writing coaches, Mary Kingcaid. I have reams of notes. In an instant, she picks out the challenge, the goals, the villain, and the dramatic arc. "I am an orphan. I'm one of 18 siblings. I escaped emotional pain by immersing myself in music." Then in one sentence, I go from International Judge (villain) and struggling to make payroll (challenge) to Elizabeth Welty and the gift of Tony Robbins. And then she says, "You simply list three strategies you've implemented that your audience can emulate." My story is 3-minutes to the second. The professionals always make it look easy.

I present my story to Bo and the group. There are approximately 25 people in the audience. Bo has only one critique: When I mime signing the payroll, I looked down at my imaginary paper. "Don't do that," he says. "Hold it up and look sideways at the audience." Never take your eyes off your audience, never lose contact.

Shortly before my second and final presentation to Bo, I have an opportunity to rehearse my talk in front of a live audience. It's the Bartell Academy's Winter Gala Recital, held at the Fox Theatre, the same theater where I'd performed Aconcagua with the symphony. I adapt my story for the occasion. This time I talk about how I found music, almost lost it because of

Mr. International, and the lessons I learned in persisting. We have over 100 students performing, so I've split the concert into four recitals. I have four opportunities to practice my speech. I am well prepared by the time I present to Bo.

Bo's references and analogies are, unsurprisingly, often sports-based. When I finish, he says, 'You know, in the locker rooms, when the guys have come up against a worthy opponent, someone who just goes out and gets the job done, someone who gets to the top quickly, that's kind of where you are. You get the job done. And that's why you're gonna make such a great business mentor and such a great speaker." I feel as if I've just achieved a 99-yard touchdown.

Amongst the participants in the program is the organizer of TEDx Huntington Beach. She approaches me after my speech, "You should apply for our 2023 speaker series," she says.

As per an assignment from Bo, I have been writing in my journal about 'things I want to accomplish.' One is to do a TEDx speech, but I had expected it to be farther down the road. Now, here it is, staring me in the face.

On the last breakfast of my final two-day intensive in Tampa, I meet with Myron to get more clarity about the direction I need to go in business. When you're inside the bottle, it's hard to read the label. This is why mentors are so valuable. By now, Myron knows a lot more about me. He knows, for example, that I'm a Tony Robbins fan. But he also has a keen insight into his students' strengths. He says, "Patricia, you've got something not even Tony has. When he stands up, this big fit, healthy, handsome man who is transforming the world, he has to convince his audience that he was once where they are. But when you walk onto the stage with your crutches, your body tells a story. And once you open your mouth, people will listen because they can't deny what you've gone through, what you carry with you. You've gone from pain to power. You know financial pain and financial power, personal pain and personal power. However you choose to frame it, I see a million-dollar empire in you, I see you on stage, and I see books, lots and lots of books..."

Myron Golden sees what I could not see, which is why we all need a mentor; someone who can call forth the destiny that awaits us.

A great mentor doesn't just show you the path but reveals the potential you couldn't see within.

GEMS OF WISDOM FOR CHAMPIONS

The world doesn't just want to know what you do. Dive deeper. Show them why you do it, and watch the magic unfold.

Challenge your limits. When faced with 'I can't afford it,' dare to ask 'How CAN I afford it?' Shift from scarcity to abundance.

The greatest stories aren't just heard; they're felt. Dive into your narrative with raw emotion and watch as walls crumble and connections form.

Don't just share facts. Evoke feelings. For in emotions, connections are birthed, and loyal tribes are formed.

Ask yourself: What story is holding you back? And what narrative will propel you forward? The pen is in your hands.

Thirty-Five

USING SELF-DEFENSE TO CRUSH IT IN BUSINESS

"To guard oneself it to also guard one's dreams, aspirations, and the empire one seeks to build."
—Patricia Bartell

"Both in self-defense and business, the greatest victories come from mastering yourself. Develop self-control, cultivate resilience, and always strive for personal growth."
—Bruce Lee

Self-Defense offers metaphor, analogy, and life skills aligned with business success. It's why so many great leaders have, at one time or another, undertaken to study its techniques.

Rob Golden, Myron's brother, is an ex-top US military man who runs a program called 'When Seconds Count.' Myron suggests I look into it, and I do. I'm Hispanic. I'm in a minority group. I'm a woman. I'm on crutches. I am potentially an easy target. I sign up with Rob, and we agree that I'll fly to Tampa early for two training days before Myron's next event.

On the first day, I arrive at Rob's office and immediately wonder what I've gotten myself into. There are almost 50 different handguns on the table. I spend the morning absorbing all I can as Rob covers topics I'd never even considered, relating to the importance of self-defense.

Afterward, we go through the handguns. "We're going to the shooting range," he says. "You need to learn to use your weapon. I hope you never have to. But if you do, you better get a bull's eye." My brothers taught me to fire a rifle on the farm, but I've never handled a handgun. As it turns out, I'm a pretty good sharpshooter. But bullets are not my interest. Far more valuable are the lessons in self-awareness. Rob explains where to sit in a restaurant, where to face, what to watch for in a crowded space, and how to detect potential threats.

A common consequence of childhood trauma is an inability to recognize 'red flags.' Children who have suffered abuse or neglect often have trust issues. They waver between hypervigilance, seeing danger when there is none, and being far too trusting when caution is called for. As a little girl, I trusted nobody. At university, I went to the opposite extreme, I trusted everybody. I had a hard time saying 'no.' I would help everyone with their schoolwork, with their social challenges, and with their personal dilemmas ahead of my own. So much so that one of my roommates, Amanda Overman, in our shared digs, immediately after graduating, before I moved in with Debby, wrote the word 'NO' on my bedroom mirror. "You have to learn when to say 'No' and when to put yourself first," she said. Rob Golden is not just teaching me self-defense; I'm learning about boundaries.

Gold Nugget

A clear and decisive 'no' can be more potent than a hesitant 'yes.' As with personal boundaries, in business, too, assertiveness saves dreams.

Security is always present at the events I attend, but I've never given much thought to the real physical threats faced by high-profile personalities. I imagine myself being dangerously wealthy and dangerously famous and jokingly ask Rob, "When I get to that level, will you be my security personnel?" He replies, not at all jokingly, "Absolutely." I hired a self-defense trainer. I got more than I bargained for: a true brother. What a gift!

On day two, we move on to my voice, and how to use it as a weapon. The Voice: far more reliable and potentially more potent than a gun, and for me, far more loaded.

Rob takes me to his office, located in a brick building with small windows and a warren of rooms. The CIA has a satellite office in this building. We go on the weekend, so it's all but abandoned. Still, it's guarded like a fortress. Once inside, we enter a room with a desk and chair. "OK," says Rob, "You sit there. Right. You're at home. I'm a Burglar. What do you do?" I grab an imaginary gun and sort of squeak, "Get down on the floor, hands on your head." Under severe stress, most people freeze. We lose our voice just when we need it the most. "Not bad," says Rob encouragingly, "but try again." I do, louder this time. "OK," says Rob, "That was your 'foyer' voice. Now let's hear your 'outside' voice.'"

I imagine that I am being attacked and victimized. But this time, my voice will not be taken from me. From the depth of my belly comes a roar that stuns me, stuns Rob, and stuns the CIA agent in the hallway, who concerned, asks Rob, "Do I need to call 911?"

I've not only found my voice, but I've learned to be loud.

GEMS OF WISDOM FOR CHAMPIONS

The spirit of an entrepreneur parallels that of a warrior. A warrior defends their land, their people, their beliefs. An entrepreneur protects their vision, their team, their legacy. Both are rooted in passion, in an unyielding commitment to stand tall, face forward, and roar.

Have you ever paused to recognize the warrior within you? The one that battles everyday challenges, risks, naysayers, and self-doubt? The one that refuses to let the weight of failures crush your dreams? The world may see a business person, but deep within, the heart of a warrior beats.

Ask yourself: How loud is your roar? When challenges arise, do you confront them head-on or shy away? Like mastering self-defense techniques, mastering your entrepreneurial mindset requires training, practice, and unyielding commitment. Your voice, your confidence, your spirit—they're your most potent weapons.

Every time you face adversity, you're training. Every hurdle you overcome, every fear you confront, every 'no' you assert— you're honing your skills, strengthening your resolve, and shaping your destiny.

Your path in business, as in life, isn't just about warding off threats. It's about recognizing them, understanding them, and transforming them into stepping stones to your next victory.

So, the next time you're faced with a challenge, hear your inner warrior whisper: "Bring it on."

And remember, the loudest roars often emerge from the silent battles within.

Thirty-Six

CRUSHING THE FEAR OF MAKING MISTAKES

"Embrace each mistake, for it is the echo of your courage and a map of your growth."
—*Patricia Bartell*

2023 is my year. I am preparing for my keynote speech. I am writing my first book. I have two TEDx talks on the calendar. In preparation, my team has mapped out a comprehensive content calendar to push my personal brand. We're shooting behind-the-scenes videos for my YouTube channel, Facebook, Instagram ... It's pedal to the metal. Patricia Bartell is on the move.

Or is she? I have one foot on the accelerator and one on the brakes. I'm burning rubber. I'm burning fuel. I'm burning out.

I've grown the social media presence for other businesses. I know what to do. I've performed for the camera countless times. I've nailed that. I've got the training. I've got the experience. I've got the support team. I've played the accordion live in front of thousands of people. So what is holding me back? For all the work I've done, for all the distance I've covered, there is something that I have not addressed. And it's pushing against my chest, demanding to be acknowledged.

I make an appointment with my mindset coach, Jeff. It's audio only, and I'm worn out, I haven't slept properly for days. So, I do the call lying in bed with my laptop next to me. I feel like a patient on Freud's couch. I laugh out loud at the thought of it, then have to explain the scene playing out in my head to Jeff. He is so still, so quiet, so calm. "That's exactly how it should be," he says. "I want you to be as comfortable as possible to talk this out." And the session begins.

I know the drill. Start with gratitude. We always begin our calls with the good things going on. I tell him that I've just today received an invitation from the Spokane Symphony to perform in their Valentine's Day Tango concert in 2024 with my group, Tango Volcado. That's the segue.

I tell him about my scheduled social media appearances. I tell him about my hesitation. I explain the brakes-and-gas-pedal wheel spin I'm in. The words are falling out of me.

"Where are you feeling this, Patricia?" he asks. "Emotions always manifest somewhere in the body. Can you locate the feeling?"

"In my heart center," I say.

Gold Nugget

Every emotion tied to a business decision has its roots connecting back to a personal experience. To understand your business decisions, understand your personal history.

And as I locate the feeling in my body, I locate it in my biography. There are 13 stairs to my bedroom in the Montana farmhouse. I'm back on the ninth step. I feel a sharp pain in my chest. I don't know what I've done wrong or why I'm being punished. Then I'm in the kitchen. It's nighttime. I feel the fear. I feel the sting of a branch against my back. I hear Barbara, clear as day, saying, "Quit tryin' to be the center of attention. Don't draw attention to yourself. Not everything is about you. You talk too much. Stop being so loud. Children should be seen and not heard."

And there it is.

"Coach Jeff, I know exactly what my problem is. I can hear it, I can see it, and I can feel it. I'm afraid of making a mistake. I'm afraid I'm gonna get in trouble for drawing attention to myself."

"Yes, he says, "and you don't know how severe the punishment will be."

To put myself 'out there,' I have to risk being judged. I'm afraid of taking a stand, of expressing my opinions. I'm afraid of being polarizing. I'm afraid to show who I am, I am afraid of drawing attention and of making a mistake. Every belief I've had to break down and rescript is being tested. I am quite literally being called on to walk my walk and talk my talk. I have to show up as my authentic self, and I have to accept that not everyone will like me, and that needs to be OK.

Gold Nugget

The most powerful shield against criticism isn't perfection but authenticity. Be undeniably yourself, and criticism becomes merely an opinion.

Then Coach Jeff asks, "Patricia, what did all that pain serve? What beauty was born from that pain?" That has always been the right question. Not, "What is wrong with me?" but "What did the pain serve?" "What is it trying to teach you?" "What have you learned?"

I thought my heart would explode; the pain was so big for such a little girl. My heart had to expand to contain all that pain. But emotion is just emotion; capacity is what counts. My heart hurt because it made room for compassion, empathy, and passion. It was making room for people with different ideas and different beliefs; it was teaching me to love on a higher level.

Gold Nugget

Every setback, every trauma, every criticism is an invitation. An invitation to learn, grow, and sculpt a stronger self.

What beauty came from an accordion teacher who was so harsh I almost abandoned my music? From him came my academy and how I choose to teach through joy and encouragement, not criticism or fear.

What beauty came from the international judge who disrupted my academy and left it on the brink of bankruptcy? From him came my journey into business and the path to growth.

Barbara took away my voice, so I spoke through music. Had it not been for the abuse, I might have played music, but I would never have pushed myself to go as deep as I did.

And from love withheld, I found my love for God. It wasn't modeled in my family, but in search of it, I found my spiritual home.

Gold Nugget

Each challenge, each critic, each confrontation is a classroom. The world isn't working against you; it's teaching you.

I end the call knowing that the past few days have been another lesson to be leveraged with my clients. I cannot truly teach what I have not experienced. I have a new understanding of my clients, of their trepidations in showing up in front of the camera and announcing themselves to the world. And I know what to tell them: The only mistakes are the ones from which we never learn, and the only people who never make mistakes are the ones afraid of trying something new.

I put the pedal to the metal. I lift my foot off the break.

GEMS OF WISDOM FOR CHAMPIONS

The world doesn't respond to what you intend, it responds to *who* you are. How are you growing internally?

Remember, my friend, the path to greatness is laden with mistakes. But those who dare to make them, dare to be great.

Let the echoes of past pains be the music to which you dance into a future full of promise and potential.

Thirty-Seven

THE SECRET TO CRUSHING IT EVERY TIME

"Beyond the confines of our known reality lies a realm of infinite potential—tune into its frequency."
—Patricia Bartell

"Tune in to the energy of awe. Feel it. Stay connected to it. Become more aware of it. Feel it. Experience it. Notice it. Relax into it. Enjoy it. More. Receive ... And who do you wanna be when you open your eyes? You have to become the person of your future; to live in that future. By the end of this walk ... it's time to become it ..."

The sun rises over the Maya Riviera on the Yucatan Coast of Mexico. We are a group, more than 2,000 people strong, and we've been up since 4 a.m., tapping into the surplus melatonin in our brains and activating our pineal glands. The sky over the sea has gone from dark to pink and gold to blue. The sand beneath us has gone from cold and damp to fine and warm. 2,000 people lying on a beach with their hearts wide open.

But this has been no whoo-whoo-chakra-opening-hand-on-neighbors-heart retreat. It's been seven days of intense lectures with lifetimes of information and hours of meditation integrating what we learn. We've discussed science on a whole new level for me: wavelengths, cells, energy, and matter beyond time and our current realities. We've been talking about creating the most empowered versions of ourselves.

The first time I hear 'Dr. Joe Dispenza,' I do my usual Google research, then dismiss him as 'the meditation guy.' It's a hangover from my religious upbringing that suggested meditation was 'new age' or 'occult.' But the name keeps popping up like a Jack in the Box whenever I open the self-development drawer. "This man's the real deal," says one person on the Tony Robbins Facebook group. "He is on another level." says someone else. I Google again. I read with more attention. I watch him on YouTube.

Gold Nugget

Your future does not lie in the replication of your past,
but in the innovation of your thoughts
and the bravery of your actions.

Joe Dispenza holds a Doctor of Chiropractic (D.C.) degree and is widely known for his work as an author of best-sellers such as Becoming Supernatural. His research takes place at the intersection of consciousness, neuroscience, and epigenetics (the study of changes in organisms caused by modification of gene expression rather than alteration of the genetic code itself.) He often explains the physiological and biological aspects behind the mind-body connection and the transformative potential of meditation and mental practices.

"Thoughts," he says, "are the language of the brain; feelings are the language of the body. And how you think and how you feel creates a state of being. A state of being is when your mind and body are working together. Our thoughts are electric; our emotions are magnetic. Together they create an electromagnetic field that draws abundance toward us. When our thoughts and feelings are positively aligned, there is nothing we cannot do or become."

Something as simple as moving into an elevated state of joy, love, inspiration, or gratitude for five to ten minutes daily can produce significant epigenetic changes in our health and body.

Like most simple ideas, the miracle is in the consistency of execution. The more you discipline your mind and body, the more you master the laws of abundance.

Every morning of the five-day retreat, I wake up with the birds and ride my electric scooter up the hill from the Maya Beach Resort to the conference center, chased by the rising sun. The day will commence by taking the focus off of me, off of my circumstances, off of the people around me, and just finding stillness. I remember the verse, "Be still and know that I am God." We're all told at the start of the retreat to 'get comfortable with uncomfortable.' But Joe has a way of building anticipation around the experience of 'meditation' I have never heard of. He makes sitting still for one hour positively exciting.

When first introduced to the idea that our beliefs inform our thoughts and our thoughts inform our feelings, I felt like a veil had been lifted. My childhood thoughts were dictated by others. Their voices were forceful, emphatic, and absolute. With new understanding, I had come to believe that the ability to evaluate many ideas, many routes to success, and many points of view was at the heart of what it means to create. I sought out spiritual mentors, business mentors, and self-development mentors. I hungered to share their knowledge, methods, and wisdom.

Lying on a beach in Cancun with my eyes closed, in a sustained period of raised vibration, I begin to paint my future and to put feeling to it. I draw it into the present. I am back on stage at

Spokane's Fox Theatre, performing in a full auditorium. This time my accordion is not the headline act. It's my crutches. They have been covered with gold leaf. They are bright, shiny, and gold! They are not a symbol of weakness; they are a symbol of resilience. They tell a story all of their own: The very things we think hold us back are the internal drivers that propel us to enormous success. My main keynote speech is called *What's Wrong With Me: From Crutches to Crushing It*.

I imagine what it feels like to see the orphanages, the schools, and the business schools I create in third-world countries. I see the crowds from the stage. To have a voice more absolute, powerful, and emphatic than those who tried to define my narrative for me. There is no symphony behind me now, no roll of the timpani drum. This is not Astor Piazzolla's *Aconcagua*. This is my song. My truth. My voice. I stand at my full four-foot-something height. The spotlight is on me.

Once, I was a parentless girl from a third-world country, in a catalog of orphans, without a picture, without a paragraph. Look at me now.

Later, when someone asks, "How did you achieve so much in such a short time?" My reply is simple: 'A hunger for excellence and the passion and drive to never give up!'

It was an insatiable appetite for life that propelled me from ordinary to extraordinary. This hunger, this burning yearning, starts with a decision to envision the life you are called to live and, with fierce determination and passion, to find a way to realize your dream.

In every endeavor you undertake, stay fiercely determined, committing not just 100% but 120% of your heart and soul. Do not sit on the sidelines and watch others live their dreams; get in the game and go after your own. As you close this book and embark on your own journey from pain to power, remember my words: 'Be hungry. Stay determined. And never give up!'

Finally, I leave you with a last piece of wisdom that has been the north star on my journey: "All things are possible with God." Mark 10:27 and "Whatever you do, do it with all your heart." Colossians 3:23.

As you journey forth, may you, too, pour all your heart into your endeavors, letting your crutches become your catalysts, your own levers of transformation, driving you towards your victories.

Remember, your trials are merely launching pads to do the extraordinary.

And, please never forget...

You are not broken.

You do not need fixed.

There is nothing wrong with you.

Your power is found when you embrace your weakness, making you unstoppable.

Stand tall. Dive deep. Rise higher. And go *CRUSH IT*!

LAST GEMS OF WISDOM

What if the greatest barriers in your life are not external but reside within the limits you've set for your mind?

Close your eyes. Replay one of your highest achievements. How does it feel? How are you breathing? What are you saying to yourself. From that point—choose your next steps. Make decisions from where you want to be—not where you are currently.

You have been gifted with the rare power of choice. Will you choose mediocrity or greatness?

In the vast expanse of the universe, remember that YOU matter. Your dreams matter. Your journey matters.

Are you living by default or by design? The blueprint to your success lies in your hands.

Feel the pulse of your purpose. The world isn't just waiting for your success; it's yearning for your unique impact.

THE 'CRUSH IT'

COMMUNICATION COURSE SERIES

(Total Value: $1,779)

Crush It with First Impressions *(Value: $297)*

Crush It with Unstoppable Confidence *(Value: $297)*

Crush It with Conversational Mastery *(Value: $297)*

Crush It with Leadership & Influence *(Value: $297)*

BONUS: Crush Emotional Barriers *(Value: $197)*

BONUS: Crush It by Finding Your Voice *(Value: $197)*

BONUS: Crush It with Brain Hacks to Learn Anything Faster! *(Value: $197)*

A Special Gift Just for YOU!

In appreciation for your trust and for picking up this book, I'm granting you exclusive access to this high-value course bundle. This is not just about communication; it's about transforming your internal and external influence.

Captivate. Connect. Close. Every. Single. Time.

Access at PatriciaBartell.com/Bonus

ACKNOWLEDGEMENTS

Writing this book has been an intense journey of reflection, growth, and gratitude. Each word, sentence, and chapter has been inspired by countless interactions and lessons learned over the years. Today, I pause to express my heartfelt thanks to those who have enriched my story and empowered me to share it with the world.

Debby, you're my personal dedication, pouring your care and faith into me. Through your nurturing guidance as both a mother and a cherished friend, this book finds depth and a joyous conclusion that endures. My deepest gratitude for your constant love for me, shielding me through the storms, and uplifting me in my pursuit for my dreams.

To Myron Golden, your breakfast meeting was more than just a meal; it was a pivotal turning point in my life. Your vision sowed the seed for my series, *From Pain to Power*. To my Sifu Dan Lok, who gave me not only the title of this book but also the clarity of my entrepreneurial path. Your influence, teachings and wisdom has been extremely profound. My journey to Crushing It began with both of you, two giants who believed in me. Thank you!

My unwavering administrative team at Bartell Music Academy has been the backbone of this endeavor. Johanna Campbell, Eli Boni, Kayla Ray, Heidi Flom, and Corrie Nosov, your dedication and commitment have given me the bandwidth to make this dream a reality. Johanna Campbell, who began as a nine-year old piano student, your evolution into a team leader has been awe-inspiring. You're not just a reflection but an extension of my ethos. Corrie Nosov, from the time you were just seventeen until now, blossoming into a devoted wife and mother of two wonderful children, you've tirelessly dedicated yourself. Your meticulous attention to the book's design and layout, your unwavering protection of my brand, and your generous spirit in taking on so many responsibilities have provided me the freedom to direct my focus. Your commitment is deeply appreciated.

Yevgeniy Nosov, witnessing your journey from an eighteen-year-old music student to a teacher and now a professional photographer has been truly inspiring. Your photographic genius has added visual life to this story. Thank you for dedicating your time and providing me with such a rich array of photo options, always delivering your best.

There's a unique bond between a teacher and their long-standing students. Marcia Lydiksen, Margaret Collyer, and Diane Guffin, your consistent encouragement and aid have been irreplaceable.

Tamara Rothbart, your countless hours on Zoom, capturing and weaving my stories together, and connecting the dots to bring out a coherent flow is beyond commendable. Your expertise and dedication turned my experiences into this remarkable manuscript.

Izdihar Jamil, your exceptional skills in editing and proofreading, coupled with your invaluable guidance during my book's launch, were instrumental in bringing my dream to fruition. Moreover, you opened the door to the TEDx world that has profoundly impacted and reshaped my life. I can't express enough how much these moments have defined my journey. From the depths of my heart, thank you.

Bruce and Reshma Allen, your unwavering guidance, encouragement, and constant reminders of God's profound love have been pillars of strength for me. Reshma, your beautiful friendship, listening ear and wise counsel have been invaluable. I treasure every moment. Bruce, writing the foreword for my book is an honor I deeply cherish. Thank you for being the trustworthy big brother I know I can always count on.

Rob Golden, another brother to me, you were the first to truly highlight the confidence I exude, even with my crutches. You saw strengths in me that I never knew. Bro, your presence in my life is cherished, and I'm deeply thankful our journeys intertwined.

A roaring shout-out to 'The Dragons' led by the King of Closing, my Sifu Dan Lok! To each and every one of you, your collective spirit, wisdom, and unwavering belief in my journey have been nothing short of monumental. Your steadfast support has not only illuminated my path but also fortified my spirit. Traversing the demanding world of entrepreneurship is an intricate dance, yet with you—visionary titans of industry—beside me, I've felt continuously seen, valued, and championed. Your blend of candid advice, bolstered by heartfelt encouragement, has ensured that I never felt alone, even during the most challenging stretches of this journey.

A heartfelt thank you to Tertius van Eeden, whose expertise in self-publishing has been invaluable. Tertius, you've skillfully guided me through complex decisions, safeguarding my journey as a new author. Your encouragement, friendship, and being my APP partner have meant the world to me. I'm also grateful to your company, Print on Demand, which has played a critical role in elevating my book to international audiences. By handling all the specifics, you've granted me the freedom to concentrate on my mission. Your steadfast support has been a cornerstone of this endeavor.

Nick Santonastasso, I'm deeply grateful for your endorsement and for paving the way for my message to reach my global audience. Your story and spirit are nothing short of inspirational.

Brian Tracy, your endorsement and the belief you have in me has left an indelible mark on my heart. Your faith in my mission fills me with immense gratitude. The joy I felt upon receiving your support was so overwhelming, it kept me awake with happiness that night!

Gilbert Reyes, throughout my evolution into the businesswoman I've become, your steadfast friendship and constant support have been invaluable. Your consistent check-ins during this book's creation and your boundless encouragement have impacted me more deeply than words can convey.

To my Tango Volcado Quartet – Jody Graves, Tana Bland, and Eugene Jablonsky, your willingness to support not just in music but in friendship has meant so much to me.

Marsha Schlangen, Laura Balbo, Selina Lopez, Theresa Jones, Laura Clancy, your support, laughter, and focus have been my pillars of strength during the emotional rollercoasters of this journey. And Shereese Alexander, your grounding presence and constant words of encouragement mean more to me than you'll ever know.

In closing, I hold a special place in my heart for Kendall Feeney. Even in absence, your legacy resonates through me, fueling my confidence and belief. You lit the torch; now I carry the flame.

To each one of you—whether named or unnamed—this book is a reflection of all of you. Thank you for being a chapter, a line, a word in this story. My deepest gratitude to each of you for being a part of this journey.

ABOUT THE AUTHOR

Patricia Bartell was born in Bolivia. As an infant, she contracted polio and a severe case of tonsilitis and was given almost zero chance of surviving. At nearly five, she was adopted and moved to Charlo, Montana, where she was raised on a farm and become one of eighteen children. Patricia overcame insurmountable odds to become not only a world-champion musician but also a sought-after keynote speaker. This led her to the prestigious stages of TEDx, where she delivers compelling talks, sharing her experiences and insights with a global audience profoundly impacting the worlds of business, music, and self-development.

Her personal story of triumph over adversity serves as an inspiration to thousands and as a manifesto

of courage, tenacity, and faith. Patricia is passionate about empowering people, be it in business, music, or life, to unlock their full potential and to change their perspective on what's possible. "Change what you see," says Patricia, "and what you see WILL change."

Her accordion performances consistently earn widespread acclaim. As the founder of Bartell Music Academy and Accordion Life Academy, she harnesses music's transformative power to shape her students' lives by encouraging them to break free from limiting beliefs, discover their unique gifts, and perform confidently and passionately.

As an internationally recognized music judge, she is in demand for prestigious music festival appearances and curriculum contributions. Her stellar reputation and progressive approach are helping to reshape the music industry.

When Patricia hits the stage as a keynote speaker with her gold crutches, you can feel the shift in the room. She doesn't just talk—she embodies resilience, transformation, and success. She commands attention on a variety of stages—from business conferences to broader platforms reaching the masses— with her invigorating tales of adversity, growth, and triumph. Furthermore, Patricia draws from her extensive experience as a business owner to integrate actionable insights, ensuring her listeners are not only inspired but are also armed with tangible strategies for personal and professional success. With her magnetic stage presence, Patricia has a unique gift as a closer. She masterfully converts her compelling speeches into opportunities, demonstrating firsthand that with determination and the right strategies, nothing is truly impossible.

Patricia's *Crush It* Business Programs empower entrepreneurs and professionals to *Crush It* on both physical stages and digital platforms, including social media video marketing, to achieve exponential business growth. Known for transforming individuals into dynamic speakers, she equips them to captivate any virtual or physical audience and radiate confidence and charisma on camera. Central to her methodology is the mastery of constructing compelling narratives that not only engage listeners but also forge deep connections, ultimately converting effective communication into tangible business opportunities.

Patricia can be reached via the following platforms:

Website: PatriciaBartell.com

Email: connect@PatriciaBartell.com

Social Media: @patriciabartellofficial

Made in the USA
Las Vegas, NV
05 July 2024

91910099R00218